As well as studying to be a coach, Ledley King now mentors disadvantaged Tottenham teenagers and acts as a Tottenham Hotspur Club Ambassador: continuing to give back to the community that shaped his life and the club that holds his heart.

Award-winning journalist Mat Snow has been a Spurs and England fan since 1966 and is the former editor of the football magazine *FourFourTwo* and music monthly *Mojo*. He has written for numerous national newspapers and other periodicals, including the official club magazine, *Hotspur*.

KING

Ledley King My Autobiography

Ledley King and Mat Snow

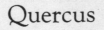

First published in Great Britain in 2013 by Quercus Editions Ltd
This paperback edition published in 2014 by

Quercus Editions Ltd
55 Baker Street
7th Floor, South Block
London
W1U 8EW

A CIP catalogue record for this book is available
from the British Library

ISBN 978 1 78206 907 2
EBOOK ISBN 978 1 78206 906 5

10 9 8 7 6 5 4 3 2 1

Text and plates designed and typeset by Ellipsis Digital Ltd

Printed and bound in Great Britain by Clays Ltd, St Ives plc

CONTENTS

WHAT IF . . . ?

One day you're primed and ready to play for your country against the host nation in the knock-out stages of one of the world's biggest international tournaments, and the next you're a thousand miles away, watching the game on TV and feeling completely torn. It's your country, they're your teammates, and one or two of them are good friends. You should be there yourself, battling alongside them.

You're willing them to win – of course you are – but if they win, it forces you to make a decision you really don't want to have to make. Whatever you decide, it's probably the wrong decision. Whatever you decide, you're going to be letting people down. Letting down loved ones, family, friends, comrades, perhaps even the whole country. And certainly letting down yourself.

I can't bear to let anyone down. I'm not exaggerating when I say my conscience won't allow it. I have always tried to do my best to pay back all the encouragement, support and belief that people have offered me and which has helped me strive to reach the highest levels.

1

So, watching that game, I cannot deny that part of me wanted my team, my country, to lose. I should have been there helping them win, but instead I was a thousand miles away, half-willing them to be beaten. Watching the drama unfold on TV, I was alone, physically exhausted, emotionally battered, gripped by tension. Every second was agony . . .

Back in 2002, when I was twenty-one years old, I won my first senior England cap. It was just before the World Cup hosted by Japan and South Korea, and it was never very likely that, with so little full international experience, I would be called up for the England squad as one of the choices at centre-back, a position that above all demands steadiness and experience.

But two years later I was ready to be tested. The club I'd played for all my life, Tottenham Hotspur, had struggled to find the best way to achieve its ambition of playing the winning, entertaining, glorious football which the fans and its history as one of Britain's very greatest clubs demanded. But as an individual player I had made progress, and that is even despite spells of injury that were becoming a bit too frequent for comfort. I was now sure I had the ability and experience to pull on the England shirt, get out there and play my full part against the best the world could throw at us.

So I felt I'd fully earned my place among the thirty-two players called up to England's pre-tournament training camp in Sardinia. We were there to acclimatize ourselves to the hot conditions we'd face when we came to the real test: Portugal, hosts of Euro 2004.

In Sardinia I got to know some of the England players as people. Off the pitch, Gary Neville was a bit of a character. He had an older head with a mature attitude. He could be opinionated, but always for the benefit of the team. If he saw something needed saying to the coach, on behalf of all the players he'd be the one to say it. Any problems, whether with the hotel or training pitch, he'd be one to raise them. And he would get the team together to find out if anything needed fixing if he couldn't see it for himself.

Then there was David Beckham. He had a friendly relationship with the coach. They found it easy to talk to each other at any time. The coach was Sven-Göran Eriksson. He was very quiet, calm and relaxed. Sven was very likeable. He made it easy for players to approach him. He also made the camp comfortable and relaxed for everyone. He let the players be adults and didn't place too many restrictions on them. They were allowed to spend time with their wives and girlfriends, going to their hotels after training, though not every day.

Sven's policy of treating the players as adults led to all the controversy about England's WAGs – the wives and girlfriends who were shopping and sunbathing and distracting the players, if you believed everything you read. In my opinion, the media made something out of nothing. Players can tell the difference between a relaxed training camp and a holiday. We're there to train and we know it, and don't want any distractions while we're actually working.

But after you've done the hard work, I don't think there's any problem spending time with your family. Not every player wants to spend time with their family during training, but I think they should have the option. Like anyone else, to do the best job possible, players need to feel comfortable. I've been in environments where players are bored, unhappy and on edge, with nothing to do to take their minds off football and the game they're preparing for. I think it works much better when players go into a game relaxed. You'll see that a relaxed team performs as a team, a real group.

And me? My girlfriend wasn't in Sardinia, but not because I didn't want her there. Three years before, I'd met Stephanie at a night out, and we started going out.

But now, while I was in Sardinia, she was back in the UK. She was seven months pregnant so it hadn't been advisable for her to fly out with me.

Back in the Sardinia training camp, not all the thirty-two players would be going to Portugal. The squad would only number twenty-three. So we weren't just training. We were competing to make the cut. And we wouldn't be told which of us had succeeded until the training camp was over and we were back in England.

In the thirty-two there was only one other Tottenham player: Jermain Defoe. He was an East End lad like me, and since joining Spurs I'd become very close to him. When I heard the news that he was one of the nine players who had missed out on selection for Portugal, I was gutted for him. But I was delighted to be involved in the squad myself and was looking forward to a great tournament, where we would be testing ourselves against really good opposition.

I had just five caps, including only one start – in a draw that February against Portugal – so I was still a novice compared to most of the England squad. Sol Campbell was a fixture in central defence, and he'd been my chief inspiration at Tottenham when I was a young player learning my trade. But alongside him, instead of Rio Ferdinand, who'd been suspended for missing a drug test and so could not take part in the tournament, Sven's next choice of centre-back was my old teammate when we were kids playing for Senrab FC, John Terry. But he was carrying a niggle, so that might give me my opportunity. Yet I would be competing for that spot with Jamie Carragher, who also had more experience than me. Realistically, though, I fully expected John Terry to be fit for the first game of the tournament, so I resigned myself to sitting on the bench – if I was lucky.

But as the day of the first game drew closer, John Terry still wasn't fit. The night before the game I was told that it would be me starting alongside Sol Campbell. We were playing France, one of the very best sides in the world. They had Thierry Henry, David Trezeguet and Zinedine Zidane. It would be a severe test. But for all France's quality, we had a pretty good team too, with Paul Scholes, Steven Gerrard, Gary Neville, Ashley Cole, Frank Lampard, David James, David Beckham, Michael Owen – and a young lad called Wayne Rooney, who was eighteen at the time but already a sensation.

As the day drew closer, I grew more and more nervous thinking about it. I was always a quiet lad who kept his feelings to himself and I didn't show my nerves even though they were bubbling inside. For me, this game was not going to be about glory. My only concern was that I didn't let anyone down. As I was a young defender with little experience at this level, all eyes would be on me not to mess up.

But I had reasons to be confident. Sol and I had never partnered as centre-backs at Tottenham, but I had played at left-back with him, so we knew each other's game. And having just played almost all the previous season in a flat back four for Spurs under the caretaker management of David Pleat, when I went into the flat back four for England against France I felt very assured.

Before the game, the coaches and some of the older players made a point of having a word with me in the changing room: 'Just play your game, and it'll be fine.' That told me, if nothing else did, that all eyes were on me. Being young was no excuse for letting the side down. This was a man's world, and I was twenty-three, a man and not a boy. Besides, Rooney, at eighteen, was a lot younger than me, though he was a striker, a player with freedom rather than one on whom the team's defence depends. On the pitch, whatever your age or inexperience, once you're out there, you're out there. You have been chosen as someone good enough to play, so if you have a stinker there are no excuses. If you have a stinker, you have to admit there is only one reason: you're not good enough; you're not ready to play at that level.

So you come out of the changing room with all the nerves. Out on the pitch in the warm-up before kick-off, it's a lovely day. The England fans are in high spirits, and so are the French. You feel the anticipation of a big game. I was focusing on getting through it without making any mistakes. If I could succeed in doing that, in being dependable, then the time might come when I felt comfortable in the England team, and growing confidence would allow me to play with more freedom.

My first real test came when Claude Makélélé played the ball and was running down the left in readiness for the return pass. But it was a little bit overhit, so he was trying to keep the ball from running out of play, and I shoulder-barged him so the ball went over the touchline for an England throw. I could hear the crowd really get behind me, which meant a lot, because many of them won't have known too much about me as a young one-club player. That successful first test of my defensive ability competing at such a high level settled me down. I thought to myself, OK, this is just another game. Yes, a big game, but it's still a game of football, and playing football is what you've done all your life. So just play.

As the game goes on, I get into it and begin to feel quite comfortable. And we're playing really well against the defending European champions, with World Cup winners in their side as well. When you play against a side of that quality your concentration level is high. It needs to be.

When we go into the lead with a Lampard header from a Beckham cross, I couldn't be feeling any better. We're celebrating in the huddle, and I feel really together with the team. Playing, and especially winning, games is what truly bonds players together in a team. The excitement of the heat of the battle gets you out of your comfort zone. I'm normally quiet, but not when I'm celebrating an England goal with my teammates.

In the second half Rooney goes on an amazing run from his own half, beats a few players, skins Thuram, runs at Silvestre and wins a penalty. We're thinking, Yes! With a two-goal lead we can win this. So up steps Beckham, one of the finest dead-ball strikers in the world . . . and Barthez, who has also played for Manchester United so will have faced him in the training ground, saves it. It's a blow. In our minds, we've lost a two-goal lead.

The game goes on, and France are winning more control, but we're standing up to everything that they're throwing at us. It gets to the last minutes, and we're working hard to hold on.

WHAT IF . . . ?

By now Emile Heskey has come on to hold the ball, and, being the kind of player he is, he's working his socks off and tracking back to try to help the team. On the edge of our box he puts in a little bit of a clumsy challenge and gives away a free kick. Up steps Zidane and whips it over the wall and into the bottom corner, leaving David James standing there. Sheer class. That's why Zidane was the best: he made the difference. Against him in a dead-ball situation, you were helpless.

Just like that, the victory has been taken away from us. We'd stood up to everything they had thrown at us in open play and put so much into the game that, the moment the ball went in, the draw we now had felt like defeat.

So we take the centre, it goes back to the keeper, David James, who boots it back into their half. Stevie G nicks it off one of their players who's come forward now that France's tails are up and plays it back to the keeper, since at this point we're playing out the game.

From where I'm positioned, I can see exactly what happens next. Thierry Henry anticipates that back pass and runs onto it. James brings him down, sending him head over heels. Clear penalty. I see it but I don't believe it. Up steps Zidane again, and we all sense he isn't going to miss.

As he steps back, he throws up. Just a little bit, maybe in the heat . . . and despatches the penalty, no problem.

It's a tough one to take. On the final whistle, the French players are jubilant, jumping around the pitch and making a lot of noise. Not Zidane. He shakes hands with each of us and walks back in. He's scored the two goals, won the game, shakes hands and is back in the changing room. A true class act.

The England dressing room was a quiet place afterwards. But Gary Neville said that, if we continue performing like that, we'd have no problems progressing through the group and the tournament. We were all hurting, but what he said made sense and had credibility coming from a player with so much experience at the top for both club and country. We *had* played really well, and if we kept up that standard, we wouldn't lose many games. That lifted us a little bit, which we needed because we had to pick ourselves up straight away to prepare for the next group game.

I'd played well against France, and some good things were said about my performance. My confidence was high, and I thought I could have gone on to play well in the next game. So I was disappointed when I was dropped from the starting line-up of the next group game, against Switzerland.

Sven didn't really explain why he dropped me. But John Terry was fit again and was selected ahead of me. Though he only had three more England caps than me going into the tournament, he would have been ahead of me for selection in defence because, playing for Chelsea, he was seen as having more experience in the top European club competition, the Champions League.

My view is that international football is different from

playing for your club. You're up against different national styles rather than different club styles. After France, I had thought I had earned the right to start another England game. But though I was disappointed and felt the manager's decision was unfair, I was never one to make a meal of it, especially at this stage in my career. And, of course, the manager is paid to make decisions, which won't all be liked by everyone.

There were a lot of players in the squad who had given up hope of playing in the tournament at all. They knew that they would never get a chance if first-pick players remained fit. This group of players were discontented because they'd been to previous tournaments and made up the numbers there as well. I'd always had the chance to play so I didn't know how they felt. I'd been disappointed by their attitude, thinking that, if you're good enough, you'll get your chance to play; and if you play well, you'll get your chance again. But they knew what to expect: even if you get your chance and play well, don't expect to play again if the player whose position you took gets fit.

For a while I didn't understand their attitude of 'what difference does it make?' Now I knew exactly how they felt. But I kept my disappointment to myself. The show must go on, and you don't want to detach yourself from why you're all there in case you're called on and find you're not mentally ready, find that you've switched off. I'd seen it at Tottenham in training, where squad members just go through the motions and aren't prepared for it when the manager tells them they are involved this Saturday. So I needed to keep myself in a state of readiness in case the chance came to perform again.

Though I wasn't started against Switzerland, I was on the bench. As a defender, being on the bench is not ideal, because generally you only go on if there's a crisis, and you're thrown into it at the deep end. So I had to be ready in case John Terry pulled up during the game and I was called on to replace him. Was I hoping something like that would happen to give me my chance? No. I wanted to be there on merit. Going on as a sub would not have taken away my disappointment in the manager for not having started me in the first place.

I was on the bench again when we beat Croatia 4-2, with two goals from Rooney and one apiece from Scholes and Lampard. I was brought on to replace Scholes in midfield on seventy minutes, so I could see that I had an important role to Sven as a versatile squad member. He brought me on in preference to dedicated midfielders Owen Hargreaves and Joe Cole, so that was a boost too. If I had to sit on the bench, at least I now had two potential doorways onto the pitch: midfield, as well as defence.

The next game was the quarter-final, taking place three days later, on the evening of Thursday, 24 June. It would not be easy. We were to face the home nation, Portugal, in the Estádio da Luz in Lisbon. It promised to be quite a night.

At six o'clock that Thursday morning I was woken by the phone.

It was Anne, one of the FA's personal welfare officers looking after us. The message was simple: Stephanie had gone into labour, nine weeks early. It was a big shock. We'd been told the baby might be early, but not that early.

I asked to speak to Sven, but they told me to wait an hour or so until he woke up. I waited. When we spoke, he asked me to tell him everything. I explained that it was nine weeks premature and my first, and that it was a hard decision but I should probably go back.

'Absolutely,' he said. 'I think you're making the right decision.'

Of course, the timing could not have been worse as far as the Portugal game was concerned. Even though I'd reduced his options at the last moment, Sven was very understanding. He said that, if we got through, he'd like me, if circumstances permitted, to come back to the team and continue to be part of the tournament.

On the bus from the airport terminal to the plane I ran into my Tottenham teammate Jamie Redknapp, who was over in Portugal doing media work. He was very surprised to see me heading home on the morning of this vital game. What's more, I was all by myself after being sheltered in the England squad with all the staff to help you. We sat together on the plane, and he helped calm my anxiety; with no phone reception, my mind kept turning over what was happening at home.

As soon as we landed, my phone was on, and I spoke to

Stephanie. The baby had been born. It was too much to process right there and then, so I didn't say anything to Jamie, just headed straight to the hospital, alone with my thoughts.

The baby was 3 lbs 4 oz – and was being monitored in an incubator. Suddenly Portugal and my sense of total involvement in the European Championship with England felt a long way away and a long time ago.

So it was even weirder when, after leaving the hospital, I was able to get in front of a television just in time to watch the second half of the England game against Portugal. I've never been so tense and nervous watching a game. When you're actually there in the flesh, as part of the team, you don't have nerves, but back at home I felt incredibly tense. And wouldn't you know it, after having a stinker of a season as a striker at Tottenham back under Glenn Hoddle, when he couldn't buy a goal, Portugal's Hélder Postiga not only scores the equalizer that takes the game to a penalty shoot-out, but has the audacity to dink the penalty that takes England to the brink of exiting the tournament, with the Portuguese keeper, Ricardo, absenting his own goal to administer the heartbreaking death blow from the spot.

So that was that. In a way I look back and think that Postiga almost did me a favour. With England out, the pressure I'd been putting myself under to leave the hospital and go back to Portugal was gone. But until the moment Postiga scored that penalty, my loyalties were being pulled in both directions.

But if not for this personal emergency, would things have been different for me? Different for England? There can be no answer to that.

It's a case of what-if. And in my life and career, there've been a few . . .

JUST A BOY FROM BOW

I was brought up mainly by my mum, Beverley King. From when I was very young my dad was in and out of my life. I'm the oldest of two brothers. Emerson came along when I was seven.

I'm an East End kid, a Cockney born in Mile End Hospital on 12 October 1980. Like most prospective parents, my mum had names on a list for both boys and girls – she didn't know in advance which would pop out! On her list for a boy were the names Ledley and Brenton. They're not family names, but ones she'd heard before in the Caribbean and liked.

Until I was four, Mum and I lived with her parents, my nan, Louise, and grandad, Joel. Being by herself for most of that time, my mum needed their help to look after me while she was at work. Sadly, they've both now passed on. My nan was a nurse at the London Hospital in Whitechapel. I don't remember my grandad working, though I know that he had done a bit of carpentry. They had both been born in Jamaica and come over as part of the *Windrush* generation, but they didn't talk about those early days much. I grew up very close to them in Carr Street, near Mile End Park and the hospital where I was born and just a little north of the River Thames at Limehouse. It had been very run down but was being re-developed when I was a kid, but I'm afraid I'm too young to remember.

Three years older than my mum, her brother, my uncle Donald, was a keen footballer himself, but I don't think my grandparents were too keen on him going down that route. Church commitments got in the way and stopped my uncle from progressing. My nan went to Baptist church, though I don't remember my grandad ever going, and at a young age I attended regularly every Sunday. I had football as well, and that won out in the end. I don't remember too much about church, because I stopped quite early. Rather than the church, I think it was my grandparents and my mum who shaped me.

My dad? His name is Herbie Patterson. He was a bad boy who couldn't stay out of trouble – petty stuff. He was away a lot when I was a kid, and there were long spells when he wasn't around. It was much better that way. When he was there, I remember a lot of shouting and screaming and even violence in the house, and the police would come around. I think some-times my mum got hurt, but as a kid you don't know the full extent. She would hide it very well.

He wasn't violent towards me, though like most black kids in those days I would get the odd slap for being naughty from whoever, including my grandparents. It was never unjust or for petty things. I always knew that, if I got a smack, I'd done something to upset them and that I deserved it. They'd be trying to spell out for you the dos and don'ts, and pave your way as a child growing up. It wasn't a problem to me back then. It wasn't bullying.

My dad's passion was boxing, and his half-brother, Rod Douglas, boxed for Great Britain in the Olympics in 1984, and was a Commonwealth gold medallist in 1986 and four-times ABA light-middleweight champion, winning the first after just seventeen senior fights. Though my dad tried to get me into boxing, putting gloves and a headguard on me and getting me to spar a bit, it wasn't really my thing. Perhaps he was trying to toughen me up. Even though I went to a boxing club once with him around the age of ten, I didn't allow myself to be distracted from what was by then my passion – football.

My dad hasn't been in my life at all since I was eleven. Though my parents weren't married, I had his name until I was ten or eleven. But it came to a point where my mum decided she didn't want his name to be associated with me, and it was better that I change my name to hers. She knew by then that I not only had a passion for football but a talent for it too, and that it was best for the future if he wasn't associated with me any more in case he turned out to be a liability.

Since then I don't think he's tried to get in touch, not even when I started getting attention as a footballer. My mum has always protected me and has wanted me to be able to concentrate on my football without unnecessary distractions and pressures. She's done a good job in keeping these things away from me, sometimes more than I would have liked. There are things I would like to have known, but being the protective kind of person she is, she would leave it to the last minute to tell me. I would ask her sometimes, 'Mum, why didn't you tell me?' But she always wanted to me to concentrate on my football and get through that game. When I was growing up, she didn't want to share everything going on her life with me because she didn't want me to worry, being the older of the two kids and so naturally the one who would take on board feelings of responsibility.

But now I'm past the age of thirty and have retired from playing professionally, I think it's time for me to talk about things more with her, to find out. A lot of my life and background is still quite closed to me, and it's a habit we've both got into. Just as all my life she's protected me from worry, I find it very difficult to bring up anything that I know will hurt my mum, to go back on memories or subjects which I know will worry her. We both hold things back to keep the other from being anxious. Now, when I go round to my mum's house I sometimes have a look round for old pictures. We don't have many, not even of me when I was very small. When I was a kid I wasn't that interested. I am now.

My early memories are fuzzy. I remember living at number 8 Berebinder House, in Tredegar Road in Bow. It's still there, a four-storey block of twelve council flats, each on two floors. There was no garden but a green area outside. There is a lot of this kind of low-rise council housing around there, mixed in with the old terraces with bow and sash windows, some with basements down a short flight of steps with another short flight leading up to the porch of the front door. Where I grew up is where the old East End which escaped the bombs and the East End rebuilt after the Second World War live side by side just off the Roman Road, home of the famous market, one of several in the East End.

My mum works as a housing officer for Hackney Council, helping to rehouse people. She's always worked and she still does that job part-time. She has lot of friends there, she enjoys the work and she's not one of those people happy to do nothing. Her work gives her a way of life.

When she was at work, I was looked after by a lovely local white lady called Peggy. There were lots of other kids so I always mixed in. I wasn't a lonely child. But I was always quiet.

When I was five I went to Olga Primary School on Lanfranc Road, about half a mile away, twenty minutes' walk for a kid. It wasn't the closest primary school to where we lived – Malmesbury and Old Ford were a bit nearer. My guess is that my mum had had a look around them all and made her choice.

I liked a lot of things at primary school. I wanted to try things and didn't dislike much. I enjoyed maths and English and got to play the violin. It was quite a laid-back school and nice to grow up in. It wasn't pushy, and I always felt safe. I enjoyed my group of friends and going to school every day. The headteacher was Ms Smith, who had a daughter at the school.

In the last year we put on a play. I think it was *Bugsy Malone*, or it may have been *Oliver!* I was not that happy with my part: it was small and not the starring role I was looking for! Maybe that's why I struggle to remember which play it was – I've banished it from my mind!

When I left Olga as the biggest kid to go to my new school as one of the smallest, I didn't feel dumb or out of my depth. I felt satisfied with what I knew. After we all left school, I kept up with a lot of the friends I used to play with.

It was at Olga Primary that very early on I met the friend who was to help shape my life. James Carter was the same age as me, and we struck up a friendship and very soon became inseparable. His family were a big part of my life growing up. I spent a lot of time at his house just round the corner from the school, where my mum would pick me up after work, or my grandparents would come and walk me home – I didn't have a bike until I was about eleven and had left Olga Primary. And sometimes James's dad Fred would drop me home in his green Mercedes, which was like a limo to me back then. Fred was in business, and when I was about ten or eleven I remember him opening up a shop on the Roman Road selling mirrors and picture frames.

Growing up, I loved the simple food all British kids love – chips, beans and sausages. I enjoyed the food James's mum Beryl cooked more than I did the food at home. Beryl was also a dinner lady at Olga Primary, and a good one! My mum would get home from work so late she didn't often have time to cook and I'd already eaten, and my nan would cook West Indian food like yams, ackee, swordfish and jerk chicken. As a kid I didn't really appreciate Jamaican food. I wanted chips, beans and sausages every day!

With my best friend James having a brother and two sisters, and the Carters being such a happy, lively family, I was really happy at the age of seven when my brother Emerson came along. I wasn't jealous at all or upset that naturally I no longer had so much of my mum's attention. We still get along fine.

Today, my brother has been to college and has a passion for music. While he's also working at all sorts of bits and pieces of jobs, he has been looking to go down the music path, putting grime and club-type beats together at home which sound pretty good to me. But people who know more about the music scene than I do tell me that it's very competitive and not easy to break into, to make your mark and make a living. It's been harder for him than for me because he's never had that one thing he really enjoys and really, really wanted to do.

If it hadn't been for football I'm sure I would be like my brother and still looking for my path. I say this to my mum, but she disagrees and tells me that I would have found something else to give me a focus and a path. That shocked me. My mother can see something in me which I can't; I really do think that if it hadn't been for football, to this day I may not have found something.

I was jealous of the Carters: they were the perfect family to me and seemed to have everything, including a dog called Sally, though I didn't have any interest in having a dog at that time, nor did my mum. For a while I had two goldfish called Rocky and Rambo: that was as good as it got for me! I loved *Rocky* when I was a kid – that was a great film. I must have been a fan of Sylvester Stallone and had help from someone when naming Rambo. Now I have a pug called Otis, who is a lot of fun. I enjoyed going round to the Carters'. It was different to my house. With James I'd go out and play football or, if the weather was bad, we'd stay in and play computer games. We didn't watch a lot of TV, which is what I did when I was at my grandparents'. My grandad always seemed to be in his chair, and I'd sit with him on my little sofa, and we'd watch all the kids' programmes after school.

He supported Liverpool, and my very first memory of professional football would be when Arsenal beat Liverpool at Anfield in the last game of the 1988/89 season to nick the title in the last minutes. Liverpool was the team of the era. I remember the Candy kit and the small shorts and really admired John Barnes. He really stood out as a great black player.

My grandad was a quiet man, didn't say too much, but was big and imposing, six foot three, similar to me. That's where I get it from! He was really kind and gentle, taking me to the park every day during school holidays. He would sit and watch while I joined in the games of football.

In school and out of school, during term time, weekends and holidays, in the playground, the park or the street, by the time I was seven, football really was the biggest thing in my little world.

THE WORLD AT MY FEET

All my friends at Olga Primary shared a passion for football. From as young as I can remember, school was all about break-time, those twenty minutes when you'd rush out into the playground and kick a ball about, with the goal drawn in chalk on the wall. Even then, hitting the wall inside the chalk and scoring a goal was a great feeling. There was another game, where we'd try to kick the ball through a hole in the fence, and when we didn't have a ball at our feet we'd be imagining football games scored according the roll of a dice. That was our idea of mental arithmetic!

At school we took football seriously in breaktime, and Olga Primary picked the keenest and best of us to play in five-a-side competitions with other schools and compete for the Smith's Crisps Cup. We really enjoyed being in the Olga Primary team. It was a chance to get out of school and go to different places, see other schools. We played after school hours, and it was a big thing to travel away from school in a minibus. We took representing our school at football seriously and wanted to win.

We were friends in the team, and though we were all East End boys we came from some very different backgrounds. There was Luke Wilson and, in goal, James Smith, but also a little Pakistani kid called Kamal. I don't think football was his thing at first, but he developed a passion for it and got better as we went on – he was an aggressive little player. A Nigerian boy called Paul Ayoge was a little Pele back then, a really small and skilful striker; he also played for a local boys team called Puma. Me and James Carter were pretty good too.

We didn't really have fixed positions, and I would play everywhere. I certainly didn't think of myself as a defender until a little later. Even when I was a few years older and still at school, I never enjoyed calling myself a defender. I never thought that position was very glamorous. When I played, I was a defender first but went forward every chance I had with the ball at my feet. I hated being pinned at the back. I felt I had too much to offer. I felt I could affect the game more from the midfield and at school would play there as well as at the back. At that age I didn't study or watch defenders either. I loved attacking players, flair players. I grew up expressing myself as a footballer.

If anyone asked me at that age what I wanted to be when I grew up, there was never any doubt or hesitation in my mind: I wanted to be a footballer. No other answer. And it wasn't just that I wanted to be a footballer. Even at that age, at primary school, I would tell people I wanted to be the best – the best in the world. Of course, back then in my little bubble, I didn't know how big the world was. But at that time, having the ambition to be the best in the world was a help, because it gave me a drive.

As I mentioned, John Barnes was a player I looked up to. You could say he was a role model. But you need to remember that, back then, before the launch of the Premier League and live coverage of daytime games on Sky, to watch top English professional football on TV you had to be allowed to stay up late for *Match of the Day* or wait for the FA Cup and League Cup finals. So, like all football-mad kids back then, I really hadn't seen very much on TV at all.

Then, at the age of nine, along came a whole summer of daytime and evening football, showcasing the best in the world. Italia '90 was the biggest thing ever for me and so many other football-mad kids back then. It dragged me in, and I never looked back.

It was very special to watch the national team play on the world stage, which all ended in the drama of Paul Gascoigne in tears. Obviously I wanted England to win, but even though they didn't, and of course I was disappointed when they went out, the characters, the games, the whole tournament were great. It was the event that cemented my desire to be a footballer. Me and my friends at Olga Primary would see new tricks on TV and then try them out ourselves, at first in private at home with a ball, then at school.

After the 1990 World Cup, Paul Gascoigne became my

favourite player. Everything about him appealed to me. There were other skilful players, but he had personality as well. He was so full of life and played football with such enjoyment and exuberance like he was in the playground. That's what stood out to a youngster.

Italia '90 was also about the winners, the West Germany of Jürgen Klinsmann and Lothar Matthäus, and the big characters like the Cameroonian Roger Milla, the Italian Golden Boot Totò Schillaci, the Colombian Carlos Valderrama with his supersized hair. They weren't just footballers, they were stickers.

I had the Italia '90 Panini sticker album and after that the domestic Panini sticker books and collected the players, badges and managers of the English and Scottish top divisions. I enjoyed collecting sticker books and trying to fill them. Sometimes my grandparents would pick me up from school and buy me a couple of packets of stickers from the newsagent on the way home. My nan would give me money, and I would also run errands for my mum for pocket money. And I would get the occasional football magazine like *Match* or *Shoot* so I could look at the players. I didn't put the posters on my bedroom wall at home, but they were still my idols.

I was also watching a lot of good players when, a little later, they started showing Italian Serie A football on TV during the era of Marco Van Basten, Roberto Baggio and George Weah. I was delighted to be watching players from other leagues strut their stuff. Back then, we didn't have Sky and access to watching

Premier League games, so Italian Serie A on Channel 4 took over for me and I grew to love that league.

When I was eleven I moved on from Olga Primary to The Blessed John Roche Roman Catholic School in Upper North Street, Poplar. Blessed John Roche was not my mum's first choice, which was Cardinal Pole, another Catholic school, though we weren't a Catholic family. My mum was looking for a school with high standards and discipline and found one two miles from my home, near Chrisp Street Market, so I'd get the number 8 or D6 bus there and back.

Blessed John Roche closed down in 2005, but when I was there it had just over 450 kids, mostly boys, because it was moving from mixed to just boys; there were only girls in the fourth and fifth years when I joined, so by the time I was in my third year there, it was all boys.

My best friend James went to a different secondary school, Raine's, but on my first day at Blessed John Roche my mum and I went round to the Carters' first thing in the morning to show me off in my new uniform of black trousers, blazer and V-neck jumper, and red tie with orange and blue stripes. It was a proud day for the Kings.

I was nervous and apprehensive that first day when my mum took me into school. There were only two other kids from Olga Primary, and we were split up, so my class was full of complete strangers. The classes were graded according to academic ability, with Ward at the top; I was in the second, Owen. Ward were the boffins, Owen was pretty clever too. Below us were Makassa and Newman, which were middling, and at the bottom, you really didn't want to be in Loyola or Clitherow.

It felt scary because the older kids were like men. At primary school I had been the tallest kid, but now I felt very small. The first few weeks I wandered around feeling lost and would often literally lose my way in the two parallel corridors. It took a while to learn the short cuts to find your way around. I'd find myself following people in my class, tagging along.

In my first year in Owen, I sat next to a lad called Tony O'Donnell, a good worker who I got quite close to. We both took pride in working hard. He was intelligent and had come to school to learn, and that attitude rubbed off on me. So, following suit, in the first year I did well and got decent grades. And in the school orchestra I was selected to play cello, probably because, though I felt very small compared to the older boys, I was a big lad as a youngster and could take it home to practise. I was pleased to put the cello between my legs and enjoyed playing it, taking part and blending into school concerts, but not so much lugging it home and back to school again.

It was all a new level of learning for me. The thing was, though, that the lads I had most in common with were the ones who played football at breaktime. Because at my new school I played football at breaktime like I'd done at Olga Primary, I became quite popular and got a lot of friends. But not many of those were in Ward or Owen.

I began to fall behind in lessons, drift in my work and slip away from Tony a little bit. But really I think I was finding my own comfort level. Halfway through the second year I had to come down a class. At first I was a little bit embarrassed, but once I was there I felt quite happy. But I was very sure that I never wanted to be in the bottom two classes, Loyola or Clitherow. The kids in those classes were seen as no-hopers even by the twelve-year-olds, winding each other up and cussing, as we'd say. I went down to one of the middle classes, Makassa. I felt comfortable there: the atmosphere and pace more natural to me than Owen or Ward, where the kids were regarded as the brains of the school. I didn't feel that was me. I felt I was a different kind of person: fun, not so intense, and I liked to relax.

Of course, that's not what the teachers said. They would tell me that I had a lot of potential – the most out of my friends – but was easily distracted. But maybe I didn't really want to be in that top group of boffins. I wanted to belong to the core group, the middle ones who played football and had a laugh.

In a way, then, my growing focus on football was narrowing rather than widening my horizons. But not totally. The first time I left England I was about fourteen. I went on holiday for five weeks with my grandparents to see the family back in Kingston, Jamaica, the only time I knew my grandparents to go back after emigrating to England.

Travelling from the airport to where my great uncle and

aunt lived in the country at night with no street lights is a memory. It was pitch black, and you couldn't see a thing. Then we had to get out and walk up a hill to their house in complete darkness, surrounded by the noise of all the insects. I was petrified. My grandparents were completely relaxed, but I wasn't.

When we got to the house, the first thing I saw flying around inside was a bat! I hated moths, and this was a moth times fifty! I immediately felt sick, and the first words I said when I met my Jamaica family were: 'I want to go to bed.' I felt sick at the thought of standing or even sitting with this thing flapping around the house. I wanted to be lying down with the covers over my head.

The next day it was very warm, and just how different their life was to mine back in London was clear when I went to the toilet. It was outside, a hole in the ground surrounded by some bricks. And there was no running water. We washed in the river.

My cousins, who I met for the first time, were so different. Even though my grandparents had strong Jamaican accents, I grew up with them and could understand them, but my cousins had an accent that I really struggled to understand until my ear got attuned. I'd brought with me a game of Donkey Kong, and they kept stealing and hiding it, so I had to keep finding it again. They had no problem stealing from me because they saw me as rich, and they had nothing; they didn't understand

I wasn't rich, and I didn't understand why they didn't have these normal things I did. They really were pretty poor.

The first week I hated being there and I wanted to go home, but after that I got used to it and really enjoyed myself. I got on well with my cousins, and we played every day. I came home with good memories of that holiday.

I've not been back, but my mum is in touch with her two half-sisters there from my grandad's previous marriage before he left Jamaica. Maybe in time I will take a greater interest in my wider family and where I'm from. But for so long I've worn the blinkers of my football career that it's been the whole world to me until now. I've not wanted anything to distract my focus, to get in the way of football.

THE HOT HOUSE

It was James's mum, Beryl, who was a dinner lady at Olga Primary, who first spotted that I had a bit of football talent. I don't know what I was doing in the playground that made me stand out against the other seven-year-old kids, but she saw something and told her husband, Fred, that Ledley's getting good and that I should come down to the football team that James was playing for. That's when I joined Senrab.

James had been playing for Senrab for about a year already, so it was just a matter of me tagging along to training and games. We were all proud to play for Senrab because we had a good team rather than because the club was famous in the world of English youth football. As kids, we didn't know that Senrab had history and was special.

It's named after Senrab Street in Stepney, where the Marion Richardson School had the pitches where the club used to train when it was founded over fifty years ago. Since then, Senrab FC has produced quite a roll call of top players and coaches, including Ade Akinbiyi, Lee Bowyer, Sol Campbell, Alan Curbishley, Jermain Defoe, Ugo Ehiogu, Jonathan Fortune, Dario

Gradi, Fitz Hall, Vince Hilaire, Terry Hurlock, Muzzy Izzet, David Kerslake, Paul Konchesky, Tommy Langley, Ray Lewington, Darren Purse, Jlloyd Samuel, John Terry, Ray Wilkins and Bobby Zamora. And in case you're wondering, Senrab is Barnes backwards: there's a Barnes Street half a mile away, not named after John, though maybe it should be.

By the time I joined Senrab FC aged seven, the club trained two miles west of its original home, in Poplar, at Langdon Park School, which had a concrete pitch under lights. We'd train on Thursday evenings at around five or six. Fred used to take James and me there from the Carters' house, where we'd go to have our tea after school. After training, Fred would drop me back home at about eight o'clock.

The first coach we had at Senrab was Paul Rolls. He was a big guy and a good coach. He loved football, and we all loved playing for the team. There was a nice family feel to it.

Was the training special? I don't think it was anything out of the ordinary for England. It wasn't like in Brazil or the Continent, playing futsal with the smaller balls to develop close ball skills. We did drills and exercises. We didn't even think of it as training, just doing stuff with the ball. But what we had at Senrab was a bunch of players who were all hungry to play well and win. Certainly at that level, the coach develops the team, but the individual has the responsibility to develop himself. Practice is everything. You get help with shooting and passing and your first touch, but ultimately you have to work on these things yourself if you're going to get to where you want to go. In my experience, it's not until you get to a professional club that you get told by a coach or manager to work on a particular strength or weakness.

We used to play matches on Sunday mornings at Wanstead Flats, just east of Leyton Orient and north of West Ham United. Fred would drive James and me in our Senrab kit: black and red striped tops, black shorts and socks, like AC Milan. We'd put our boots on in the changing room and get out and play. And after the game there was the burger stall for a little treat.

Even though we used to win almost every game, we didn't realize at that young age how good we were. We won just about every trophy there was to win, league and cups.

James was a very good player at that age. Jlloyd Samuel was a left-winger, very tricky with a lot of flair, a bit like John Barnes. I didn't have as much flair with ball control and dribbling skills as some of the players. I had size and speed and tackling. I was difficult to get past, like a rock at the back. Bobby Zamora, who scored a lot of goals, was there, and along the way Paul Konchesky joined too.

Joining perhaps two years later than me was John Terry. His family was from further east in London, Barking. He played in midfield back then and was quite short, but he had a leap on him and was great in the air. Even then he was like a little man, quite tough, and would put himself about on the pitch – and he had a voice! He'd pull us about, and we responded and did what it took to win. He made a big difference as a midfield general. You could definitely tell John Terry had leadership qualities. I don't think anyone would have said the same of me. I was shy and quiet. We were all different but we got on well.

By the age of ten or eleven, all the different parts of the team had come together, and we were almost unbeatable. When you're winning, it's always fun. Senrab was the place to be; everybody in London and the South-east wanted to play for us.

Well, nearly everyone. There were different leagues with different teams in them. Among them was another East End boys team, Puma, which, because they were in a different league, we never got to play. In my Olga Primary School team, Paul Ayoge also played for Puma. And so did this lad who moved across the road from the flat where Mum, Emerson and I had moved when I was aged, I think, ten, in Parnell Road, just round the corner from where we lived before in Tredegar Road. That lad's name was Ashley Cole.

Ashley and I go way back. Outside both our homes were football cages with iron goals in them, and there was a big group of around twenty kids aged twelve and thirteen, who played games in these football cages. It's what we lived for. So Ashley and I got to know each other.

Though at different schools and different football clubs, Ashley and I did get to play together, because we were both picked to play for our local boys teams, Hackney & Tower Hamlets and London Schoolboys. Back then Ashley wasn't a left-back but a striker, a prolific goalscorer, small and nippy with a great left foot. Because we played for the same sides as kids, we never really got to test whether he had the beating of me as a defender. When he started playing left-back for Arsenal I was shocked. Obviously they saw he had potential in that position and developed it. Of course, he still had the attacking instinct, and it took him a while to improve defensively.

Though I never got to test myself as a defender against Ashley back when he was a striker, there was a future professional opponent and then Tottenham teammate who I got to play against back in my Senrab days. Over the other side of the Thames, dominating a league in South-east London and Kent, was a team called Valley Valiants, and, apart from a very good player called Billsy, they had another star we'd all heard of – Scott Parker.

Because Valley Valiants were the best boys team south of the river and Senrab the best in the north, a one-off game was arranged to showcase the best versus the best and decide which was the best of both worlds. This was massive for us. After an hour the score stood 0-0, and at that point our manager decided to take off James and me and put on two triallists. We lost 2-0. James and I have never forgiven the manager because we think that, had we been allowed to stay on, we would have won. Losing that game of the best of the best still hurts. It was a big thing, and Scott Parker, who was on the winning side, remembers it well too.

By the time I hit my teens there was a lot of football in my life. After Olga Primary I played for the Blessed John Roche School team as well as Senrab, then also Hackney & Tower Hamlets and London Schools. With all the teams I was playing for, sometimes I'd play matches on both Saturday and Sunday, and sometimes even two the same day. But I really enjoyed it. You didn't get tired, you just kept playing. At least we didn't have to train at school or with London Schools, where matches were more occasional, but Hackney & Tower Hamlets trained on Saturday mornings. Like Senrab, it was quite serious but had a nice team feel to it.

I got to know a lot of James's friends from his school, Raine's, who played for Hackney & Tower Hamlets just as did quite a few from Blessed John Roche. Our two schools were quite competitive, and it was nice to mix together in Hackney & Tower Hamlets and try and do well.

With Hackney & Tower Hamlets schoolboys we went to play in a tournament in Florida, my second time out of the country after the family holiday to Jamaica. The team had a great chemistry, and that made the trip even better. I was abroad having fun with my mates. Parents came too to make sure that we were all right. We were all looking forward to seeing America at first hand rather than just on TV and in the movies. It was a big, big thing for all us fourteen-year-olds.

We went to Orlando and played three or four local sides then travelled to Clearwater. Back then, football played by that age group in the States hadn't developed to anything like our level, so we found the games quite easy, winning the tournament final 13-0! Our coach, Gary Northover, brought along a really, really good player called Wayne Gray from Camberwell in South London, so he really shouldn't have been playing for us at all north of the river. Wayne was signed to Wimbledon and was a prolific goalscorer. In Florida we played nine games all in all and he scored, I think, forty-five goals. They really couldn't handle him at all.

Though the opposition wasn't ideal, we enjoyed winning and the warm climate. After one of the games something happened which has stuck with me ever since. As I was walking off the pitch, one of the Americans watching said to me, 'You're the best player I've ever seen in my life.'

The holiday was great even though for me our trip to Disney World was not the highlight it was for my teammates because I am not keen on thrill rides. I really do feel that something's going to go wrong and I'm going to die! Not nice! To this day, those rides don't thrill me at all, and back then it was only peer pressure that got me on board – I didn't want to be the only one who wouldn't go on. In all the pictures which people took of us on the rides, I have my eyes shut tight in terror!

My mum, who flew out with us, had some family who didn't live far away, so they all came over and we had a get-together.

That meant I had to miss out on a team trip to another amusement park. I wasn't too disappointed!

Though quite a few lads from my school played football for Hackney & Tower Hamlets, football was not the first sport at the Blessed John Roche. That was athletics, and at school I was a 400 metre runner, and we used to compete at athletics against a lot of different schools. I don't remember getting beaten in races so I must have been pretty good.

Even though I did well, I didn't really enjoy athletics. Athletics used to scare me. It was nerve-racking being on my own on the line. I felt very exposed. As a youngster there was no fear like it. A lot of my friends felt the same way. Athletics was hard. At the same time, like a lot of footballers, I like to test myself on an individual basis, to see how good I am one on one, combat level. For all my nerves and shyness, I've always had that very competitive streak. Even though I was scared to death of competing, something in me made me win. Before a race we'd all ask each other our times, and many runners' would be faster than mine, and I thought they'd kill me. Yet somehow I always won. Something in me thrived in the battle. I could feel the adrenalin, and afterwards I felt good. But the terror in the build-up before the race was not good.

Because I had a reputation as a runner at schools level in East London, I was actually invited to run for Belgrave Harriers but in the trial I finished about fifth or sixth. That was another level up from me. But by then I had invested too much of myself in football to be disappointed. I was enjoying it too much to allow anything else to get in the way. Maybe I didn't allow myself to enjoy anything that would get in the way. I loved football, and there was no reason to change.

At that time the professional club I supported was Millwall. That's because Fred Carter was a Millwall fan and he took me and James. Fred instilled Millwall into James, and because he was my best friend I followed suit.

Back then they had some good players – Teddy Sheringham, Tony Cascarino, Kasey Keller and Terry Hurlock. It would have been nice if I had more positive memories of Millwall with those great players, two of whom I would get to know much later as teammates. But my first match was very uncomfortable for me – because of the colour of my skin. I couldn't say for sure I was the only black person there in the crowd, but we were very few and far between. There was a lot of racism around me in the stands, even from the kids. Not only the opposition's black players would get it, but Millwall's own black players too.

That was the first time in my entire life I'd encountered racism. There hadn't been any at school or the area I lived. It stopped me enjoying myself going down to the Den. I didn't get any abuse or dirty looks myself as a fan, but it was the racist abuse dished out to the players that made me feel very uncomfortable. For that reason, I used to go hoping there would be no black players on the pitch just so I wouldn't have to hear any racism. Funnily enough, the one time I got my wish and there wasn't a single black player on the pitch, the referee was Uriah Rennie. Here we go, I thought, and sure enough he got the dog's abuse. And nothing to do with his quality or lack of it as a referee either.

It was kind of James and his dad to take me, and I felt embarrassed that inside I was feeling so uncomfortable, so I never said anything. I don't think Fred realized what it was like for me; I suppose he was so used to it over the years he didn't notice. In the end I started making my excuses so I didn't have to go any more when they asked me.

But neither James nor anyone else in the Carter family treated me as any different from one of their own kids. For that reason I never worried that they might be racist, even though the team they supported had a lot of racist supporters. What I didn't know was that Millwall had far more racism at matches than most clubs. I'd never been to watch football at another professional club and I suppose I thought that *all* pro fessional football matches were like that.

I hated that racist atmosphere, but it didn't stop me from wanting to be a footballer. And now the world of professional football was entering my sights.

THE ORIENT EXPRESS TO TOTTENHAM

At Senrab from round about the ages of nine to fourteen we started to train at Leyton Orient, the club most local to our regular match-playing base in Wanstead Flats. They were the first club to grab us. Fred knew the ins and outs of what was best for me and James as players with real potential, and I just went along with things. After all, I didn't have my dad around, and my mum was busy working and she trusted Fred's advice.

Fred would give me and a lad James and I had become friends with at Senrab, Stephen Mills from the Isle of Dogs, a lift to train with Leyton Orient on Tuesday evenings. Their training facilities were in Leytonstone, a big Astroturf pitch with different age groups all training there. We used size-four balls, and the stress was on ball skills, control, dribbling and technique, more technical stuff than at Senrab, more about developing us individually. Nicky Shorey was the same age as me, and we'd train together; his dad Steve was a coach there. Games were few and far between. And at that stage there was nothing about diets: chips were still the food of choice. We were so active, playing football at every opportunity, that there was no danger of putting on any weight.

Meanwhile, Fred was busy behind the scenes. He believed James and his two friends, Stephen Mills and me, had a potential beyond what Leyton Orient would be able to develop. He had a little word with Spurs' head of recruitment, John Moncur, and, at the age of fourteen, James, Stephen and I were invited to train at Tottenham. And not just at the club's training facilities but in the stadium itself at White Hart Lane, back when it had an indoor carpeted ball court. You'd go through a turnstile, up some stairs and into a changing room.

As you would expect at one of the world's top clubs, the facilities were a lot better than Orient's, and to a teenager they had a good feel. The indoor carpeted ball court was like a large school gym, with the goals two metal frames. Compared to the facilities now it's not much, but at the time it was very impressive. The parents and friends could look down on us train through a window. My mum was very busy, though, so didn't come to see me train there, but Fred would be there watching James, Stephen and me.

We were Tottenham Associated Schoolboy trainees, a two-year deal from fourteen to sixteen, and after that, if we progressed well, we could be offered a Youth Training Scheme deal, like a football club apprenticeship. We'd get two pounds' travelling expenses from school. I travelled with a lad from my school who was already training at Tottenham, Wesley Jones, still a good friend. We'd all go to a caff on the Tottenham High Road for sausage or bacon sandwiches before games, which I don't think the youth team would get away with now.

In the first year at Tottenham the schoolboy coach was a little guy called Colin Reid, a nice man who'd played at a decent level and had also trained the West Ham youth players. In those very early days with Tottenham, we had no contact at all with the senior players, not even in training when we moved from White Hart Lane to Chase Lodge, Spurs' training ground in Mill Hill, far up in the very north of London, where the suburbs fade into open fields. While senior players trained in the morning, we trained in the evening twice a week. But sometimes the club would give us schoolboy trainees match tickets to see the first team play, and that really brought home how long the road was. These were real men, and we were still boys. We were in awe of their size and strength. But you're wearing the same shirt and feel part of the same cause. We watched the senior players not as fans but as kids looking up to the level we aspired to reach ourselves.

We'd only play matches in the school holidays, against schoolboy teams from Arsenal, West Ham and other London clubs. Tottenham Schoolboys was pretty settled as a team. It was the first time I met Peter Crouch, Narada Bernard and then, a little later, Alton Thelwell. Alton turned up three months or so before the YTS deadline and he was so impressive with his hunger and work rate that even though he trialled so late, he managed to get in; he was very well developed as a kid, muscles coming out of his ears: you've never seen anything like it. We were all from different parts of London, but together, wearing the Tottenham badge, we had a good laugh, and there was a real team chemistry. We all became good friends.

As a coach, Colin Reid was quite technical but also liked players to express themselves. After Colin our coach was Bob Arber, who'd played for Arsenal reserves, and, following his time in the Spurs coaching staff, went back to work for our North London rivals' academy scouting set-up. Bob was quite old school. He introduced a lot of running to get us fitter and liked a player to have drive, determination and spirit. For a young player, his style of management was a bit scarier than we were used to and impressed on us that this was where the hard work started and it wasn't just fun any more. With all the running, it was quite nerve-racking for me, touching your fingers on the start line like I did at school. Nobody wanted to be last in the race, nobody wanted to be seen as unfit.

Though there was no weight training – I think because, aged fifteen or sixteen, you're not at your final point of physical development – the club was looking for big players more than technical players. We had a lad called Dean Harding, who was a technically brilliant player on the ball, like a Xavi or an Iniesta, but he was so small. It was drummed into him and into us that he was too small to become a professional footballer, and he didn't get his YTS place.

Would Lionel Messi have made it as a YTS at that time? Had he been English, he certainly would not have developed as the same player. He wouldn't have been allowed. Back in those days we were told to pass and keep it simple rather than try to beat the man. Without using and practising those skills every day, you'd lose that part of your game. Of course, passing and keeping it simple are good skills too, but part of being a good manager is to see the different skills that different players have to offer, and working to develop those strengths.

In 1996 I was part of the Tottenham U16 team that went to Coleraine in Northern Ireland to take part in the annual pre-season Milk Cup tournament. I was aged fifteen, still at school, and playing in the year above my age group. Five of us school-boys were asked to go along with the first-year apprentices: Peter Crouch, Nicky Hunt, Narada Bernard, Gavin Kelly and me. We all knew each other, having trained twice a week together, and it was a big thing – both an honour and a challenge – to be asked to join older players who we didn't know. It was our first time together as a proper group, and the five of us shared a room to take care of each other, all getting on like a house on fire. Being the kids in the squad, we had a tough time from the older players and even the coach Bob Arber. They made us get up and sing a song, 'My Girl', that hit from the '60s by The Temptations.

The Spurs team did well, beating Crewe, and Bayern Munich

2-1. The weird thing was that the German giants had an English boy playing for them; his name was Owen Hargreaves. You wondered why he was playing for a club in Germany and not in England. Later in my career, at England Under-21 level, I met him again and realized that we'd played on the same pitch before in that tournament. Like me, Owen would have figured much more for his country had he not been so blighted by injury.

In the final we beat Blackburn Rovers, who had David Dunn. It was great to win something, and the Milk Cup was seen as a good, tough competition to do well in. Watching the final, the Irish fans – kids three or four years younger than us – put us winners on a pedestal. We signed autographs and felt famous. We were wearing the famous lily-white Tottenham shirt too, so that added to feeling like a star.

Straight after the final the organizers held a disco which all the team attended, and we went straight in in our tracksuits with our medals round our necks like superstars. That felt good. Stan the kit man, a lovely guy, was there to chaperone us, at the disco in his football boots. I think even he was having a good time too.

Playing in front of fans was not completely new. With Hackney & Tower Hamlets and London Schools we'd played in front of spectators, and in stadiums too. Playing on a professional pitch makes a big change from what you're used to as a youngster, and in front of spectators, even a few, it is quite nerve-racking. The jump from thirty or fifty people watching to 200 in a stadium adds to the pressure. Even playing in an empty stadium felt new. The pitch was bigger than a park pitch, and everything felt much further away. But at no point did I struggle. Like I say, at that age you can run all day.

Halfway through my two-year schoolboy contract, Tottenham offered me a three-year YTS professional contract to take effect when I left school at the age of sixteen. The club had seen what I could do and how I was developing as a player and they must have been confident that I had the ability to progress and so wanted to have me under professional contract as soon as possible rather than wait until the end of the two-year Associated Schoolboy period to make a decision, when I might be approached by another club, and Spurs would risk losing their investment in me so far.

It was a huge boost for me, but it also marked a sad parting of the ways with the friend who since we were just little kids had been such a part of my life and whose family had looked after me and set me on my path to a football career. Just before he turned sixteen, my old friend from Olga Primary, James Carter, left Tottenham. He wasn't progressing the way he'd hoped. He did go on to play for Gillingham for a couple of years, but I think he'd really fallen out of love with football. The older he got, the more the passion began to ebb away.

It had almost happened to me too. Between the ages of fourteen and fifteen, I got a little bored of football. I'd been playing almost non-stop since I was seven. And at school I was making new friends. At school I was always easily influenced, though I was never a bad kid. But there were other things going on in life. Like girls. I got distracted a little bit.

Because I had that YTS professional contract ready to take effect when I left school, that final year at Blessed John Roche felt like marking time. I continued to go to school but wasn't that engaged. I would bunk off the odd day, not to get up to mischief but because not going to school during term time was a new experience. When we didn't feel like going into school, Wesley Jones and I would meet up nearby and get on a bus to a different area and just walk around, enjoying the freedom of not having to sit in class.

Wesley was losing interest in football, what with girls and things, and some of that had rubbed off on me. But with Wes it got to the stage where he was missing training. We'd both turn up, but there were some days when we didn't feel like it, and there was a little period when we'd just walk around the area and look at girls instead.

We were stupid to think the club wouldn't notice we were going missing. The Tottenham youth coach Colin Reid called Wes into the office and let him go. And then he spoke to me, telling me that Wesley and I were distracting each other, and Wesley had been let go. But I was being given another chance to refocus. I think Colin Reid sensed that, though Wes and I distracted each other, I was the one who was easily led so I would be given the opportunity to get refocused without distraction.

It was a warning that, if you wanted to get on, you couldn't mess around and get distracted. And Colin wasn't the only one to set my thinking straight. I'd told my mum that I was getting bored of football, and she suggested that I take a year out. When she put it like that, I realized that there was no way I could just stop for a year, and that helped me to refocus too.

From that moment I didn't look back. Because football came naturally to me, I felt that working hard at it and trying to develop my full potential was something I could do for my mum. I really wanted to make her happy, make her proud. She had done so much for me all my life, and it was time to start repaying her faith and support.

Yes, football was natural to me. I didn't have to think too much, I just played it. But at that moment I realized I still had a long way to go. I was beginning to understand that there were other kids who were good at football too, and there were older ones who were better, so the road was long.

TURNING PRO

A huge milestone on the road to a professional football career came on 3 August 1996, two months before my sixteenth birthday. That day I signed registration forms for our Division Two Junior side in the South East Counties League, and, to take effect at the start of the next season, my three-year professional club contract. Also putting his name to the document was the Tottenham chairman, Alan Sugar, the first time I'd met him. He also autographed a Tottenham book for me, which is at my mum's house; she was with me in his office to countersign the contract because I was still not legally an adult. I played my first Division Two Junior game for Spurs a month later, 1-1 at Reading. I officially joined the full-time Tottenham Hotspur staff as a trainee in July 1997.

I'd had an agent looking after my interests since I was fourteen or fifteen. As he had been on my journey from Senrab to Leyton Orient to Tottenham, Fred Carter was my guide and go-between (James was still training with Tottenham at that point). Fred would have fixed things up with my agents. I've been with Jonathan Barnett and David Manasseh of the Stellar

Group ever since. Stellar's Johnny Whitmore is in touch with me and looking after things day to day.

In your first year as a YTS trainee you copy the second year, who show you the ropes. There was a lot of banter and rivalry between the two years. In the year above me was a kid called Jamie Sinclair, who also grew up in Bow. I later got a lift with him. But they weren't all Londoners; there was a boy from Ireland and a couple from up north. There was a good team spirit among them, but the second-years had no outstanding players who went on to senior success. From time to time some of the better players were called up to play with the year above, the U17s and then the U18s. Throughout my time I mixed between the two. And my first year as a YTS was also when I played my first Tottenham reserves game.

Signing my one-year YTS contract and then three-year professional contract was a financial milestone too. I was on £42 a week! I had a bank account, and the money went straight in. We also got £160 per month travelling expenses, which effectively doubled your income.

Because James had left, there were no more lifts to the training ground in his dad Fred's green Mercedes. We trained Monday to Friday and played competitive matches on Saturdays. A typical weekday for me back then would start with the alarm clock going off at seven. I'd get up, shower and have a bowl of cereal. All our kit was kept at the new training ground, Spurs Lodge, so the only thing you'd need to bring was your washbag with toothbrush, toothpaste, deodorant and creams. At Bow Road station I'd meet Stephen Mills, who'd also been offered a YTS contract, and we'd be on the tube at eight, to the new training ground all the way out at Chigwell in Essex, changing at Mile End station from the District to the Central Line. Sometimes we'd meet other trainees along the way, like Peter Crouch travelling from Ealing and the goalkeeper Gavin Kelly from Uxbridge, also in far West London, Narada from Harrow and, handily from Stratford, Alton Thelwell. We were going in the opposite direction from the rush-hour commuters heading to the centre so we could sit down and chat.

From Chigwell station there was still a long old twenty-minute walk down Luxborough Lane before getting to the training ground. Occasionally you'd get a lift from players driving past once they'd seen you around and knew you by sight. We'd be there by nine. The club was strict on punctuality, and at first you had to be smart as well – trousers and shoes, not jeans and trainers.

The seniors trained on the pitches nearest the changing rooms, treatment rooms etc, and the juniors on the further pitches, meaning that the juniors would have to walk past the senior players on their way to train. When you arrived you had chores to do; there were bibs to be laid out and balls to be pumped up to the right pressure (you can tell by touch when they're right) and loaded into the big sacks, twenty-odd at a time. We had other jobs to do, like washing up the lunch dishes in the canteen after training. When I started at the club aged fourteen, the dietary revolution was still to hit Tottenham trainees. But by the time we graduated to the training ground at Chigwell, the canteen served pasta and meat, and our diet improved without us particularly thinking about it. And by the time I was getting into the first team the coaches were getting very interested in what young players were putting into their bodies. For us players, it took a bit of adjustment to that way of thinking about dietary self-discipline.

Another chore for the trainees was putting the kits into skips and taking them to the kit man and cleaning the senior pros' boots and taking them to the players. So we were around the senior players, but didn't dare talk to them. We were kids, too shy and quiet to get involved.

There was a rota pinned up with your name against the jobs you were doing that day. Bob Arber was in charge, and he was our manager to see if we had a problem. But at that stage we were all scared of Bob and didn't want to get in trouble with him. It was tough love. For a lot of us, it was our first experience of someone who got angry and shouted at us. It was a shock at first, but we accepted it, though if someone got shouted at, the lads would have a little giggle when Bob had gone. There was no arguing back.

We enjoyed each other's company and had a lot of banter and practical joking. The biggest joker was Peter Crouch. When he was asked later on what he would have been if he hadn't been a professional footballer, he replied, 'A virgin.' That's Crouchy for you. As a group, we all loved football, loved training and would still be out there after the training session had finished, playing for fun. We couldn't get enough of each other's company and really had a love for each other.

Among my generation of Tottenham apprentices, the main group who all enjoyed a bit of fun together as well as the football was Crouchy, Alton Thelwell, Narada Bernard, Ross Fitzsimons, who went on to play for Norwich, Stephen Mills, the goalkeeper Gavin Kelly and me.

After training, we didn't want to go our separate ways so we'd find things to do, like search out a snooker hall and play pool. Sometimes we did nothing but hang around after training at Chigwell station just to be together. Sometimes for hours! That's the kind of spirit we had. None of us had permanent girlfriends, none of us had ties, and football and the team were the number one things in our lives. OK, we weren't innocent, we weren't monks, but we really were totally focused on football. And of course, being young lads enjoying the banter and the jokes, sometimes we'd get silly and get into trouble. But that was us. We were all into garage music and, though we weren't out every night, we'd hear about events and go clubbing all over London. Crouchy took us to places around Ealing where he was from; he had a few moves, but the Robot came later in his career.

At the end of the month we got paid and we'd get the train

into the West End together and go shopping with what little money we were paid, which in the first YTS year was all the same, like I say, £42 a week. Mostly we'd shop for clothes, a pair of jeans, a coat. It was a treat for us after working all month, and this was the first time any of us had earned any money. During breaks in the season, the bunch of us in the main social group would go on holiday together, the first time to Tenerife.

The group expanded all the time because we'd have friends outside the team, even outside football, who'd come along. I'd still keep up with James Carter, but when he met his girlfriend we drifted away from each other a little bit. We remained friends but we were no longer inseparable as we had been since primary school.

Aside from the main bunch of us, there was an Irish lad, Ciarán Toner, who also got a professional contract. He was a hard worker with a good attitude and an eagerness to learn, improving year after year, which is what the club was looking for as well as ability.

There was another couple of lads, Simon Clist and Ian Stone-bridge, who went on to Bristol City and Plymouth Argyle respectively, who were very different. They were bright, intel-ligent guys, quiet lads who didn't seem to enjoy having a laugh, and we felt they were different to the rest of us, like when I was at Blessed John Roche we'd felt about the kids in the top house, Ward. They were outsiders.

During my time Tottenham had high hopes for a combative, stocky but strongly built and skilful midfielder called Nicky Hunt. But he didn't progress as hoped and at the end of his two-year YTS contract he was not offered a professional contract. Most young football apprentices in the end fail to go all the way, even those with the biggest and best professional clubs. Disappointment is the risk you have to take if you seriously want to be a professional footballer. The fact is that most don't make it.

Even in the youth team, we identified completely with the club. If the results for the first team were going badly and things didn't look good for the club on the back pages of the papers, then we felt it too. Unfortunately, this was the time when Gerry Francis's early success as Spurs manager had faded, and he was replaced by Christian Gross from Switzerland. I remember him turning up with his tube ticket 'to the dreams'. That time was a blur for me, so I don't recall much first hand, though of course we knew the media regarded him as a bit of a joke. But I did get the sense that his methods didn't really click with the players, so he didn't last too long. And with his famous ticket, I don't think he helped himself in establishing the authority he needed to win over the players who'd never heard of him before he arrived.

We trainees wanted to see Spurs doing well. We wanted to be able to boast that our club was one of the top clubs around. And at the training ground every day, it made our lives easier if the first team was doing well. Even though in the training ground the first team and the youngsters trained far apart – the seniors on the top pitch, the apprentices on the bottom – you could still feel the tension when things weren't going well for the first team and they needed results. It was scary enough collecting boots from the senior players to clean. You wanted them to be in a good mood. Some days you'd walk past a player and not get a hello.

But some players were nice. David Ginola was a nice guy, always friendly and happy. And Ruel Fox was friendly – but heartless at the same time! He could really slate you, but that he was abusing us meant at least he was talking to us. Ruel Fox was old school and liked to put the youngsters in their place from time to time. But once you got to know him, he was fine. Later on our paths began to meet as I started to break out of the reserves into the first-team squad and he started to play more in the reserves. I learned then that he was a joker, great fun to be around. I like him a lot.

Les Ferdinand was a nice guy to be around. He's from West London and connected to Narada Bernard, who lived in Harrow, and I think their families knew each other. It helped if you had ground like that in common. Finding those things in common was how we grew more comfortable with the first-team players. That is why the English first-team players were the ones who became friendly first with the youngsters. Some of the foreign players still struggled with the language barrier.

Sol Campbell liked to talk to the youth players and was always interested to find out about our backgrounds. I think he took a liking to a few of the boys from the East End, Stephen, Alton and me. But you couldn't say that he took on a mentor role with any of us. He was always quite reserved and thoughtful in how he spoke to you. He didn't share too many jokes with us. The fact that you shared a word from time to time was as good as it got; a little conversation was a treat. That's how we were brought up, and we never disliked any senior player because they didn't want to have much to do with us.

Back then was a very different era to today. Things were tougher for the junior players than they are now. There was much more of a divide. And to an extent I think there *should* be a divide between the junior and senior players. You don't want the kids getting too familiar, too comfortable before they've done anything to earn it. They should be in slight awe. They should even feel a little fear. But nowadays the kids in the youth teams are very comfortable around first-team players. I hope they still feel respect and know that there is still a struggle ahead to get to that level. We had that back then.

As Tottenham youth first years, we went to Spain for a three-game tournament. We played Barcelona and Real Sociedad and Brondby.

Playing Barcelona was an eye-opener for us. They were unbelievable, just like the team now, tika-taka. They had a rhythm, a flow, a style of play that you could tell had been coached from a very early age. We'd never seen anything like it, seeing that Barça style for the first time, doing to us what they do to teams now, making angles, finding space and constantly moving. It was the biggest football lesson we ever got – they probably had 85 per cent possession, and we hardly got a kick.

But we had Crouchy and we won 1-0! Early in the second half, a big cross went in, and he beat the keeper in the air. Other than that, we hardly got out of our area and couldn't string three passes together because they kept coming at us, passing us to death and getting to the edge of our box with ease, looking to score the perfect goal. But we managed to defy the shot or the last pass with a tackle or a boot in to block, and ultimately they lacked cutting edge. Their style was totally different to the English hustle and bustle we defenders were used to, and we had to concentrate hard on reading their passing and movement. With our backs to the wall – even Crouchy was playing centre-back – we made last-ditch tackles and showed our spirit, and they learned something too: that English teams are tough to beat. It was nice to say that we'd beaten Barcelona, even though we joked among ourselves how much of a beating we got technically. In the knowledge that there were more talented teams than us, we had a good spirit and a good work rate, which stood us in good stead.

One other thing about that Barcelona youth side. After the

game both sides had a meal together, sat at separate tables placed side by side. And some of their players made racist gestures. I was wound up, and so were most of my teammates, but we managed not to show we were provoked and kept our discipline and dignity.

In that tournament, we ended losing 2-0 to Real Sociedad, who had more cut and thrust about them. So we came away knowing Spanish youngsters were good players. And ten years later, as seniors, they overtook France and Brazil to prove themselves the best in the world.

That tournament was a really valuable part of our footballing education. All the time we were absorbing information on different types of football and different types of player. It was great to learn. But playing in this tournament was not my first taste of how other countries played football. By then I had already played for England.

YOUNG LION

It's just like you'd imagine. There, posted through the letterbox at home and lying on your doormat, is a letter with the famous three lions crest on the envelope. You open it, and inside is an official letter from the FA inviting you to attend an England trial.

I was fifteen and naturally I was chuffed and proud; it was something to tell your friends. At the same time, I felt it was no more than another step on my path, that letter being something for my mum to keep as a souvenir rather than for me to treasure forever. But I wasn't light-hearted about it. I was scared. I would have to go away on my own and play with people I didn't know.

When I was fourteen I'd had trials to go to the FA's School of Excellence youth academy at Lilleshall, when it was regarded as the country's crème de la crème training facility. For a teenager showing outstanding football promise, it was the best player development and coaching you could get, even better than at a top club like Tottenham. Once you'd trained at Lilleshall, it was expected that you'd go back to your club in the fast track to become a top professional. If selected as a schoolboy, you'd go to Lilleshall for two years between the ages of fourteen and sixteen, with schoolwork on top of training.

Lilleshall is 160 miles from London in Shropshire, so it was residential – a boarding school. I'd got to the last stages of the trial and selection process, but I told my mum that, if I got picked, I wasn't sure I wanted to go. I didn't want to leave home and be away from my mum. But my mum said that, if I passed the trial, she would make me go, and I could only come back if I really didn't like it. As it was, I didn't get through. But, as an outsider to the Lilleshall group, I was still called in with two or three others to play games as an England Schoolboy.

My first game as an England Under-16 was against Spain, as I recall. You went up the week before the game to Lilleshall to train with the rest of the team, and even for only a week I didn't like being away from my mum. I'm a homely person and felt I had to be the man about the house with my mum and younger brother Emerson. Lilleshall trainees there for the full two years had their own areas, but guest players like me would have individual rooms in an annexe. Even for a week I found it quite difficult because of missing home. I just had to get on with it. But I had nice surprise when my agents at Stellar flew my mum out to Spain, and having her around really helped.

Before the game I was nervous. Also in the team was my

old opponent from the Senrab versus Valley Valiants game, midfielder Scott Parker, who was being trained at Lilleshall. Then there was left-back Kevin Richardson from Sheffield Wednesday, striker Franny Jeffers from Everton, and from Arsenal there were Lee Canoville, Rhys Weston and the goalkeeper Stuart Taylor. It was the first time I got a taste of playing with top players from different clubs, players seen as the best at our age in the country. They all knew each other, of course, but for me as an outsider both training and playing the game was nerve-racking.

At least I wasn't the only one. There were a few others. We outsiders all felt a little bit the same; we wanted to show the ones who'd been picked for Lilleshall that we were good enough, that we were on a par with them.

But the Lilleshall lads were better players than me in some respects: they were more organized on the pitch; they knew their jobs. In training there was a lot of focus on team shape and your position, in my case how to play as a defender, where you should be in a given situation. That was the week when it became clear that centre-back was really my position. This was it: no more midfield. Or so I thought at the time.

Also, now was the time for me to stop relying on raw talent and learn properly everything I needed to know to play in my position. That's when I began to look at centre-backs more closely. I learned a lot from watching people. There are the basics, but on top of that so much about being a centre-back is decision-making, doing what seems right in that moment. Watching top centre-backs, you picture yourself in their position and compare what they do with what you'd do in that same situation. And where you see centre-backs make mistakes, you learn by studying that bad decision what to do when the same situation arises for you. That way you hope you don't have to learn from your mistakes in a game because you've already learned from studying another player's mistake the right decision to make.

You also have to study players who have the same basic materials as you do yourself. When I was in the youth team, among the Spurs seniors I looked closely at Sol Campbell, and among great overseas centre-backs I studied Lilian Thuram, Marcel Desailly and Paolo Maldini. Like me, they were comfortable on the ball and had good pace.

I think that any young player who wants to improve must use all available tools for self-analysis. I think it's important to review your play on video if you possibly can. You need to see it because you can't always remember what happened on the pitch because when you're out there things happen so quickly. On video I've seen mistakes I've made, especially as a younger defender, which have shown me a solution to avoid making that mistake again in the same position.

For years now, when I watch football, I ask myself what would I do in that situation and try to learn from that process. And when I was not playing football, I liked to watch it to learn from other people's mistakes and good play what to do or not do myself on the pitch.

Watching yourself playing on TV, you realize that often what is said by the ex-pros and other pundits who've just seen the game on screen through the eyes of the TV cameras misses out on the exact reality of what happened, especially when it focuses on a mistake. The bigger picture, which often the cameras miss, would reveal why a mistake happened, how it might have been triggered by another player out of position or making a mistake two moves before. You start dissecting your team's and your own mistakes, and as you get more experienced you look for the bigger picture to explain mistakes.

As well as studying the top players in my position who shared my speed and size, and mistakes on the pitch you didn't want to make yourself, I needed to work on those basics.

As a kid I wasn't the most physical player and I needed to toughen up. A little barge with the hip or shielding the ball with your arm against the other player was as physical as it got for me. I probably played too nicely, but you learn some of the tricks. You can make a clean tackle but leave a little bit of physical contact behind that will make them shy away in the rest of the game. You can go up for a header cleanly but lean your body on them, knowing they hate that, and it will put them off their game. You learn these tricks and who they work against as you progress in the professional game. They're certainly not things I would ever have thought of as a young player.

I was slim in my upper body but always had big legs and strong hips, so I could barge with my glutes. I still had to develop the attitude to be physical when needed, but also the judgement of when not to be as well. It's not always beneficial to be in a physical battle. There's more to defending than battling; there's an art.

I would play against strikers who liked to talk and pull you about, but I very, very rarely got wound up – I got stoked up. I would not lose my temper but keep the anger burning inside me, resolving that from this moment you don't get a kick. But I never, ever saw myself as an old-school clogger. I never wanted to be horrible or to commit a foul. To me, fouling an opposing striker is a sign that a defender's been done, outsmarted. I always wanted to stay on my feet. If you turned me, I would chase back, and keep coming back at you. You might outsmart me once, but probably not twice.

These are the things I learned over the years about how to play as a centre-back. That I still had an awful lot to learn at the age of fifteen was one of the lessons I picked up as a guest at Lilleshall.

Not just technically more accomplished, the Lilleshall lads were more mature as people too. And that's perhaps because I had never taken control of my football. From an early age,

I'd left it in the hands of Fred Carter until James left Tottenham and I had to find myself a little bit.

That week at Lilleshall was good for me. I went back to Tottenham improved as a player and with my confidence boosted by having gone away and represented my country. Around then I signed my first boot deal, with Adidas, who I've been with ever since. It was another stage in becoming a real professional footballer.

Travelling to Thailand with the Under-16s was an eye-opener. It was April 1997. We had time to walk around, relax, do a bit of sight-seeing and shopping, haggling for a few fake pieces. I came back with a belt and a wallet, but for us England lads it was all about mastering the art of haggling and getting a little bargain. I have a picture of me and Nicky Weaver going for a walk in our England shorts and T-shirts. Everything was very different, especially the food. That was my first taste of being away with the England lads representing my country. It felt good.

I played with that group quite a few times. Yet the funny thing is that, if you look at those England Under-16s, with all that training, maturity and confidence-building, not many with the obvious exception of Scott Parker went on to become regular Premier League players. And though Jermain Defoe, Michael Ball, Michael Owen, Joe Cole, Scott Parker, Sol Campbell, Jamie Carragher, Wes Brown, Andrew Cole and Ian Walker were also Lilleshall graduates, the far greater number of talented fourteen-year-old footballers who did those two years of intensive football training yet failed to make top-flight careers for themselves afterwards is the reason why the FA shut down the school in 1999. It just wasn't working well enough in its stated aim of creating generations of young English players who would go on to be able to compete consistently with the finest in the world like Brazil, Argentina, Germany and France.

Why not? I have a theory. It was because Lilleshall graduates were expected to go straight to the top of the game, maybe that expectation exerted a pressure that held them back. Maybe it was luckier for me to be living at home instead, just popping in to train and play now and then.

Once you get to that level, you become expected to make it. That's a terrible pressure. There was this kid I played with for England whose name probably won't mean anything to you, and it's best if I don't reveal it. To me he was a great, great player, one of the best we had in that team. Once after a game I walked into the players' lounge, and there was his dad crucifying him about the game, and the lad was crying. It was too much at that young age. I saw how that kind of pressure could stop him going forward, and make him fall out of love with the game. For the parents of young players, it's a thin line: how do you help and support your son without piling on too much pressure?

It was lucky for me too that my mum had work commitments and didn't really understand football and so was not a constant presence at games. When, a little later, she did come and see me play, knowing she was watching made me nervous. I always wanted to play well, but I put extra pressure on myself because my mum was there watching me at last. I told her that I didn't want her to see me and think I'm rubbish, and she laughed. Obviously, having got to a certain level, I wasn't going to be rubbish. But I felt the pressure of her presence watching me after all this time. I wasn't used to it. Her not watching me play for years was a freedom for me.

I continued to play for England after turning 16, on through the age levels. I was proud to be getting picked. It was an honour to play for my country. I was the only Tottenham player at that age being picked for England, and I tried to do my best for the good name of the club and to show we had some good players.

I played six games for the Under-17s and three for the Under-18s. I remember Joe Cole, a lad from West Ham called Izzy Iriekpen who played at centre-half, Jonathan Woodgate, Wes Brown, Seth Johnson, who was then at Crewe, Jon Harley, who was at Chelsea, Darius Vassell, and Crouchy broke in too. A few of them had by this stage played for their clubs' first teams, so I knew them from seeing them on TV.

In the England team, I was one of the quiet ones who kept himself to himself. The bigger personalities tended to be the ones who had been playing for England longer and had more caps. You could spot them as soon as you joined the group. What also made a young England player comfortable was having teammates from the same club. Until Crouchy got in, it was just me from Tottenham; once Crouchy eventually broke through, it made life a lot easier for me to have a mate I could be around.

Yes, putting on the England shirt was pressure as well as pride. But if you wanted to progress, you had to deal with the pressure. The best at soaking up the pressure would make it through. I just had to hope I wouldn't crack.

THE SCHOOL OF HARD KNOCKS

I now felt that in my age group I was the best player at the club. And the year above as well. When I trained and played for England, I was tested. But at Tottenham I felt comfortable. And at that age you don't want to feel too comfortable. Fortunately, at Tottenham, there was always a higher level to aim for and test yourself against once you got there.

Pat Holland took over coaching in the second YTS year. He was old school, and talked about the West Ham players who'd been his teammates, especially Bobby Moore. I got on well with him, and he took a liking to me, I think because I was from the East End too.

As I progressed out of the youth team and into the reserves, Chris Hughton was the Spurs reserves manager. And then he was moved up to first-team coach, and I didn't play long for the reserves either before being picked for the first-team squad. Chris helped me because he'd been a defender. At the different stages of development, Chris, Pat and Bob Arber all had a big impact on my development as a player.

After playing eighteen games for our Under-17 side, I made

my debut in the Under-18s in May 1997 when I was still six-teen, and at the start of the following season, still a month off my seventeenth birthday, I scored against Leeds as part of the Under-19s' three-man defence. In March the following year I made my debut for the reserves in the Football Combination in a 2-0 win at Ipswich.

At the end of the 1997/98 season I was named Young Player of the Year, winning the club's Sydney Wale Challenge Cup. It was a huge honour and a boost, especially when the youth-team boss Pat Holland, who made the award, likened me to the great Bobby Moore because of the way he said I was so composed on the ball and could pick out a front man with a pass out of defence. There is no greater compliment you can pay any defender in the world, and it was not lost on me. I have always worked hard to try to justify and repay the faith that so many people – my mum, Fred, my coaches and, a little later, the Tottenham fans – have placed in me.

Though I was boosted by this recognition and confirmation of my own feeling that I was the best player of my age at the club, there was nothing easy about my progress through the ranks that season and into the next.

The South East Counties League was replaced by the FA Premier Youth League (Under-18) in 1997 and, the following season, the Premier Academy League U17s and U19s. As kids we never knew too much about Chelsea, but Arsenal and West Ham had really good youth teams back then. We played them both quite regularly and knew them well. Both clubs had better youth players, better teams, than we had, which wasn't great to have to admit about our two nearest neighbours.

Even at that age the players for the two North London giants had a good rivalry. I hate to say it, but Arsenal were a lot better than us. They were well ahead at that age, and we used to take a few beatings off them. Though they had the flair players, we had the bulldog team spirit and we'd fight for each other.

In 1997 a mixture of the first and second years found ourselves playing our North London rivals in a two-legged final to decide the winner of the FA Premier Youth League (Under-18). The first leg was at White Hart Lane, in front of the home fans looking to see the up-and-coming stars. It was on Sky TV as well, so it was a big deal. But nerves got the better of us, and we didn't really perform, myself included. We lost that game 2-0. The second leg at Highbury we won 1-0, chasing the second goal which would have brought extra time, but it didn't come. So we ended runners-up to a more talented side but came away from that Highbury game with a lot of pride restored, having beaten them on their home patch.

Like with the fans of the two clubs, there are a lot of friendships between Tottenham and Arsenal players, even though that friendship is based on rivalry. At Tottenham we got to know some of the Arsenal players. My friend from Bow, Ashley Cole, was at Arsenal, and over time that friendship led to friendships between a number of his teammates and mine in the youth sides. Off the pitch we got on well, and sometimes his group of friends who played for Arsenal would meet up at a venue with me and my friends who played for Tottenham. But on the pitch we badly wanted to beat each other for those bragging rights.

After the two years as a YTS, everyone the club signs as a professional goes into the pool of players eligible to be picked for the first team. There would be something like thirty-five or so professionals. That meant that there were a lot of professionals at the club who were not getting picked for the first team. In that pool of players above me pushing for the first team were Mark Gower, Luke Young, James Bunn, Paul McVeigh, Paul Mahorn and Rory Allen. When you see the good players in that pool not making the first team, you realize how difficult it will be for you coming up as a youngster. To get from the youth to the first team meant you had to overcome a lot of obstacles, and it was a difficult time.

It's even harder for a central defender. You have to to compete for a position where size and strength is important when your body may not have reached its full development. And a defender is just like a goalkeeper: when you finally get to play with the big boys, you can't afford to make mistakes. Not even one. Any mistake you make will end in conceding a goal or at least a goal chance. And as a young player, your inexperience means you're going to make mistakes.

That's the main difficulty in trying to integrate a young

defender into the first team – you've got to really trust him. For that reason a defender is not going to get his chance in being called off the bench and onto the pitch unless you really need him. But a young striker can come off the bench just to rest or replace the first-team striker even when you don't need a goal. And if the young striker happens to score, he will have impressed. As the manager, you will feel able to risk bringing on a young striker from the bench to make his debut with the first team far more often than you will a young defender. Strikers therefore get more opportunities to play in the first team.

Though centre-backs often come in pairs, and an understanding between centre-backs is important, at the youth level the coaches aren't thinking of partnerships, nor are they looking for matching pairs of centre-backs. Especially in the second YTS year, youth-team coaches are looking for individuals in whatever position who they think have a real chance of making the first team. And if they identify those players with real first-team potential, they push them hard. The fact that in the first year of my professional contract my pay jumped to £350 a week told me that the club saw me as having first-team potential, and that they also saw I was working hard to fulfil it.

So I played with various different partners at centre-back. And nothing wrong with that. If I ever got my chance to play in the first team by coming off the bench, I would have to adapt to whoever I found myself playing alongside. A good part of my training and development was about being ready for that challenge. Ready to slot in smoothly so the defence is not disrupted. So ready and so calm under the pressure of being thrown in at the deep end that the other defenders don't have to worry about my positioning or covering for me. Basically, ready for anything.

Trying to get noticed to break into the first team, you weren't just playing a waiting game. You were training hard every weekday, and playing games on top. That's a lot of mileage.

Generally, the players who cover most ground are the midfielders. Forwards and centre-backs, as you would expect, cover less ground but about as much as each other, given that the centre-backs track the opposing strikers. Full-backs cover about the same, depending on whether or not they're expected to get forward to support attacks.

Funnily enough, in our team the player who covered the most ground was a striker, Peter Crouch. I was surprised when I saw that stat later on and started watching him closely. It's not just due to the length of his stride but the fact that he was constantly moving. If the ball was played from the back to one side of the pitch, he'd pull away to the other to make himself available for the diagonal ball across. He was always running round to get himself into good positions. But back in the youth team we didn't have any technical data; we just judged with the naked eye who were the good runners and who weren't.

Training every day from the time you leave school at sixteen puts a big load on your body. Everyone's body is different, and intense training can affect different people in different ways. Some players would break down completely, and other players never get injured at all. That's how it was in the youth team.

Starting with my YTS year, I suffered the first of my injuries. I had never been injury prone. In fact, up to that point I'd never suffered a single injury. I was a total stranger to the sponge! But when I joined Tottenham I picked up a few little injuries. The first was a tear in my hip, or so I thought, which kept me out for four or five months. But the truth was that nobody knew for sure what the problem was. It was one of those mystery injuries. A player had gone into me, and in the jolt, as I twisted away, something went in my hip.

I struggled with it for a while and couldn't get it right. I could walk only slowly and had to stop training. For five months, every time I tried to come back, it wasn't right. After a while the club flew me out to Italy for specialist treatment, which was a series of injections. In the end it was just a matter of being patient, of treatment and rehab, but mostly just of doing nothing and waiting. And in the end it began to feel right again. During those long months I never doubted that I would come back from this injury, and I did.

Just as my first injury, to my hip, was caused by me twisting away from the impact rather than the impact itself, generally I was never injured by a kick or other contact. My injuries all came from twists and turns. During this period I started to experience problems. I was picking up little injuries and niggles that were taking their toll on my body. But when fit, I was doing well and showing I had potential. Waiting and getting over these injuries meant this was a frustrating period for me.

Most frustratingly, in the first team there were a few injuries at centre-back among the regulars of Sol, Colin Calderwood, John Scales and Ramon Vega. My friend Alton Thelwell was called into the first-team squad for West Ham away, and sat on the bench. Obviously I was happy for him but I was also jealous.

When would my opportunity come?

DEBUT!

Bit by bit, your opportunity approaches.

Occasionally in the youth team, individual players would get called up to train with the seniors, and sometimes on a Friday before a match the whole team would get called to play against the first team. We would be there for half an hour or so to test their free kicks and corners and also general play ready for the next day.

It was a chance to impress. We would notice sometimes the manager, George Graham, coming down to watch half an hour or so of the juniors training after the end of the seniors' training session, so it wasn't as if he knew nothing about us. Even so, we couldn't be sure we were getting his full attention compared to when he was actually taking a training session with the senior players that involved us, seeing us up close and getting a sense of our different personalities.

The first time it happened we were training on the bottom pitch as usual, and Bob Arber told us to move up to the top because we'd be training with the first team. We trudged up a bit nervous but also a bit excited in anticipation. We got into our team shape with Gavin Kelly in goal, Narada Bernard to my left, Stephen Mills at right-back, and Alton Thelwell beside me. All of us, back four plus the keeper, were good friends, and we were comfortable with each other. In midfield there'd be Ross Fitzsimons and Nicky Hunt, and up front we had Crouchy. This session was for the first team's benefit, to get their rhythm and their shape, and not for ours. When George Graham wanted to stop it, he would, and we'd go trudging back.

In these training sessions with the seniors, I felt sorry for our full-backs. Millsy had to deal with David Ginola and Narada with José Dominguez. The full-backs would come away from these sessions a bit down. Not only was Ginola a really tricky winger but also a big guy; Millsy was slight, so Ginola would throw him about and have his way with him. While Narada was nippy, so was Dominguez, and he would give him a tough time. Their confidence was knocked by trying to cope with these two senior players, and on subsequent training sessions together you could tell that, unlike the rest of us, our full-backs weren't looking forward to it.

As a centre-back, I was up against strikers like Les Ferdinand and Steffen Iversen, both of them bigger and stronger than I was at that stage. It was a good test, and not so one-sided that I went away feeling down.

In the youth team, we all knew that George Graham was a tough manager and a tough man. We were used to tough coaching from Bob Arber. Bob was old school and would tell it like it was, and George Graham was like that too. As I got to train with the first team regularly, I got to understand him and what he wanted from his players. He and his assistant, Stewart Houston, were both passionate Scots and wanted to win. George Graham liked his players to be men. He was tough even on the young players, demanding quality and the right attitude. Whether you were young or old, if he felt that what you were doing wasn't good enough, he would let you know in front of everyone. You would get shouted at and then you'd hear the other players having a little giggle.

That might discourage some players in theory, but as a young player you accepted that this was all part of the game at such a high level. And the high level is where you wanted to be, so accept it and learn from it. George Graham was hard but he was fair. He didn't bear grudges or have downs on players. You were learning, and when the managers dig you out, this was what life was about. It was only after playing under different managers and different kinds of manager that you realize that it doesn't always have to be like that. But this was how George Graham was, and as a young player you were not going to argue or give back any gyp. It was a little knock to the confidence, but you had to pick yourself up and make sure you didn't make the same mistake again in the same situation.

Players not mentally strong enough to hack it would not progress but those who could would improve. Like I say, I was a quiet lad and didn't look too far ahead. I took each training session for what it was, hoping I'd done my best and that was that.

Of all the managers I've had, George Graham was the one, above all, who really wanted to work on defence. He wanted his defenders to work comfortably with each other as a unit. He helped me understand my position. One training routine had the back four working together with me watching, then I would be called in to replace one of the centre-backs or even a full-back and sometimes even a midfielder. George Graham always used the imaginary rope linking the back four, so if one of the back four had to move sideways to defend the goal, we'd all move across as if we were roped together, keeping the same distances between us and not letting gaps open up. It was nothing I hadn't heard before in the youth team, but it was a lesson that never loses its importance for a defender.

You also need to study the play of the defenders alongside you so you understand and work with the movements they prefer. And as a young player training with the first team, you need to get comfortable talking to them and even shouting at them. For me, as someone who was always quiet, this was difficult. But in defence you have to communicate. And the senior players demanded it; they needed you to tell them what was happening when they could not see it themselves. So I had to overcome my natural quietness to be able to do my job properly on the pitch, which was good.

Towards the end of the 1998/99 season I'd sat on the bench a few times but hadn't been called on to play. You wouldn't find out until the Friday, the day before the game if it was on a Saturday, that you would be travelling up with the first team. On the fringes, you're never sure whether the player you might be replacing through injury is fit or not to play until after training on Friday, so it's very much a waiting game. To be called into the first-team squad tested your nerves because, if you made it onto the pitch, you would be playing without the friends you knew inside-out from training and competitive games together.

Most of the senior players were a lot older than me. Of the younger regulars in the first team at the time I was first called, Luke Young was fifteen months older than me, so that wasn't too intimidating. I also felt comfortable with Stephen Clemence in midfield, who was less than three years older. I got nervous before every game, and in particular when it was all unfamiliar. Thrown in with senior players who'd been there, seen it, done it and got the caps to prove it was as unfamiliar as it could get for a lad who still lived with his mum. Although striker Chris Armstrong was a lot older than me, he always made an effort to help younger players relax and feel comfortable.

Match day routines also helped build the confidence of the younger players so they'd feel comfortable with the prospect of playing a real match with the seniors. For home games, we would meet on the morning of the game at West Lodge Park, a hotel in Hadley Wood seven miles north-west of White Hart Lane, and a lot leafier and more suburban. Coming up from Bow felt like a journey to another world too, though it was only thirteen miles. I wasn't driving at that stage, so I would get a cab.

At the hotel we'd have a little bit of a chat, when George Graham would read out the starting eleven and then the substitutes. Even if you weren't named you still had to prepare yourself mentally to play in case there was some kind of accident or other unforeseeable problem before kick-off, like in the warm-up, which meant that you might find yourself on the bench after all. Like I said, normally defenders would only come off the bench to play if there was an injury or red card to one of the starting back four. Defenders would never go on as impact players, and while it was possible to bolster a back four with another defender if you were under siege, I was never called on for that reason. I cannot remember in my time at Tottenham ever going to five at the back.

After George Graham had read out the names, we had lunch at 11 or 11.30 – pasta, chicken, fish, potatoes – then drove down to the stadium in our cars to get there at 1 to 1.15. Because I didn't drive, I would get a lift from one of the other players, usually Les or Sol. Sometimes players would forget that I didn't drive and jump into their cars and disappear, so it was cringe time for me when I had to ask a player for a lift.

I didn't have too many false starts of being called into the squad without actually playing before I actually made my first-team debut. It was 1 May 1999. Tottenham had won the League Cup at Wembley back in March, but our League form was not great, and we would finish eleventh in the table. Our fourth to last game was away to Liverpool, so we travelled up to Anfield. After training on Friday, we went from Spurs Lodge in Chigwell by coach to Stansted Airport and flew up that afternoon, and at the other end got another coach to the hotel. In my time at Tottenham, playing away against Liverpool or Everton, we would not stay at the same hotel every time. Different managers like different hotels. You'd check in around six, and eat at seven.

Afterwards in the evening you'd chill out. The rule was not to leave the hotel. Whether anyone did I couldn't say, even for a little walk. Me, I wouldn't dream of it. Some players would have massages or treatments if they needed it. I was always one for relaxing. Once I was in the hotel, that's where I'd stay, feet up. I didn't get lonely. After you'd eaten and were back in your room about eight o'clock, you'd wind down in front of the TV or DVD player. Before you knew it, it was bedtime.

The senior players wouldn't share rooms – each of us would have a room to ourselves. Back as junior players when we used to double up on away trips, I'd share with Alton Thelwell. He used to call me Ledley the Lizard because he said I was always so dozy!

The following day, match day, you got up and had breakfast together between eight and nine o'clock. That wasn't optional. Then back to your room for a little while, then at around eleven we'd meet for a walk for a bit of fresh air, then back to the hotel to name the team and subs and go through the opposition with maybe a bit of video footage. When the team and bench are named, if you're not called, you will see people's heads drop – you'd come all this way but wouldn't be getting involved. It was natural and OK to be disappointed as long you didn't bring anyone else down and distract the team. We'd have brought around eighteen players with us, so with eleven starting and five subs, two players would be surplus to requirements. But they couldn't go home. You never knew whether a player might pull out at the last minute through illness or a freak injury.

At Anfield I was on the bench, and to be at Anfield and warming up on that carpet of the pitch was great, especially for someone like me, who'd grown up as a kid with John Barnes as a hero, Liverpool consistently the best team in Britain, and the Kop the most famous fans in the country.

At kick-off, on the bench, I was always anxious. I knew that all it took was one incident and you could be thrown on with very little warning. You'd not started the game with the other players, and if you come on, you're on your own. And you're cold. As a young defender, you'd almost rather not go on. If you go on, you can't afford to warm yourself up and feel your way into the game; just one mistake could be disastrous. Worse still, if you have to go on when the ball is out of play because your team is defending a free kick close to goal, you're dropped right into the deep end. Where do you go? Who do you mark? You have to avoid making any mistakes at this critical point when you've only been on the pitch a few seconds.

It's very different for forwards – they're always raring to get off the bench because they're looking to score.

Anyway, against Liverpool we get off to a flyer and are shortly 2-0 up thanks to Steffen Iversen and a Jamie Carragher own goal. But then, just before half-time, our left-back, Mauricio Taricco, gets sent off, and Stewart Houston, deputizing for George Graham, who is away, tells me to warm up. My boots are on already, so it's just off with my jumper. Running down the touchline in front of the Liverpool fans is daunting because, of course, I'm getting a lot of grief to put me off. You have to block it out.

In the half-time break, midfielder Stephen Clemence is withdrawn, and Stewart Houston sends me out for the second half to tuck in at left-back. I'm right-footed, though naturally decent with both feet, so it doesn't really bother me being played out of my first-choice position. I could play anywhere in defence and even in midfield; the only positions I couldn't play was striker or in goal.

The whole of half-time my heart is pumping – at last I'm making my first-team debut. But we're down to ten men for

Moths and bats terrified me, but who doesn't love a duck? Me, aged two.

Me aged two.

Me aged three. Was my top trying to tell me something?

Me aged five.

Aged seven at Olga Primary, where I learned to love football.

Me aged eight. Football aside, I had other strings to my bow!

Me aged nine. Crazy shirt!

Aged about eleven with my little brother Emerson (and parrot).

Left. Aged 11, a proud first day at the Blessed John Roche School.

Above. Celebrating my mum's fiftieth birthday, 2011.

With my brother Emerson and first haul of football trophies.

Above. My grandparents, Joel and Louise King. They helped bring me up and I miss them.

Left. A second mum to me, Beryl Carter, who spotted me as a playground football star.

Tournament winners Senrab FC included future stars Jlloyd Samuel (yellow sleeves) and (above him) John Terry. I'm the tall, shy kid!

Aged fourteen around the time football was taking me to a tournament in Florida.

Above. In the Spurs youth team next to Peter Crouch, with Alton Thelwell (second row, third left), Johnnie Jackson (sitting, first left) and John Piercy (sitting, first right).

Left. Aged seventeen, outside my old Bow home in my first Versace suit and Gucci loafers. I've just signed my first professional contract and life is good!

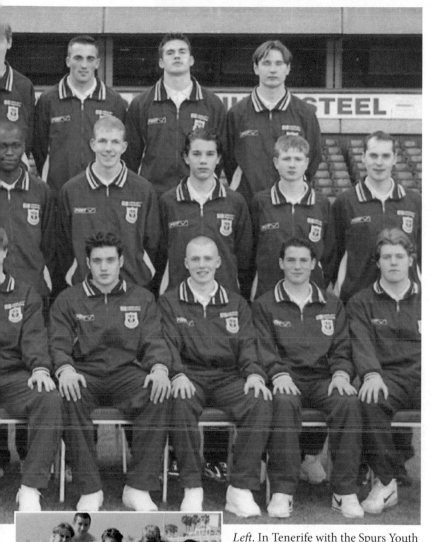

Left. In Tenerife with the Spurs Youth team. My first lads' holiday, with Crouchy providing the biggest laughs.

Left. My first-team debut as a second-half sub against Liverpool at Anfield in May 1999 was not ideal: down to ten men, we threw away a 2-0 lead.

Below. Nightmare on 1 June 2000: I break my metatarsal again in the final seconds as the England U21s lose to Slovakia.

an entire half. For the first five or ten minutes I feel the spotlight on me, with everyone looking at me to make a mistake. I'm up against Liverpool's David Thompson. The first thing I notice is the pace of the game, and it takes a while for things to settle and for me to accept that I'm out there and playing – so calm down! But we're under siege for the whole of the rest of the game, and it's tough. I'm not a natural left-back, and Liverpool keep on coming. Clawing us back one goal at a time, they win 3-2.

After the game everyone was a bit down, especially me: I felt responsible because it all fell apart during the half I was on. Regardless of the game I'd had, which flew past, and I really couldn't judge my performance, I felt disappointed in myself because when I came on we were 2-0 up and when the game finished we'd lost 3-2.

Going home, we did our journey there in reverse, with a coach to the airport in Liverpool, flight to Stansted and coach to Spurs Lodge in Chigwell. It was a sombre return, and I really didn't want to talk to anyone, whereas when you win it's all jokes and happiness on the way home. While I felt low and didn't want to talk, other players didn't take long to snap out of the gloom of a defeat and would be on the phone straight away as normal. It's down to the individual how you respond to defeat. If after losing a game I was having a chat with someone and found myself having a laugh, I always felt I shouldn't be, even though the game's gone and there was nothing you could do about it. And throughout my career in the first team, if we lost, I wouldn't look at my phone and read any messages.

Back at Spurs Lodge, we each made our way home, for me back to my mum's in Bow. I didn't watch *Match of the Day* that night. In fact, I've never enjoyed watching myself on TV, especially games I don't like, generally because we'd lost. I would record those games and only watch them when I felt ready, in my own time and by myself.

Liverpool at Anfield was my first-team debut and also last game with the seniors that season. It wasn't an ideal start. Once I had got the result out of my system, I was happy that I'd got my first game out of the way, made that crucial step.

So, mixed feelings. Though I didn't know it, that was to be the story of my career.

THE MILLENNIUM BUG

That summer me and the boys in the youth team and a few other friends flew off to Ayia Napa in Cyprus and ran into a bunch of Arsenal players there. Ayia Napa was the place to be back then for young footballers, in fact young people, full stop. We were all enjoying life. Having made my first-team debut, I enjoyed my holiday all the more. I had a sense of achievement and felt proud that I'd been blooded. It was what all we young players had been striving for since our football careers had begun. And my mum, brother, family and friends were proud that, at a young age, eighteen, I'd played for the first team. Life was all the sweeter.

My self-confidence was never so high, but as far as public recognition was concerned, nothing changed. I certainly was not being recognized and stopped on the street except by hardcore Spurs fans. That was fine by me. I wanted to be a top professional footballer, not a celebrity.

I now felt I was getting close to regular first-team selection. But I had one worry at the back of my mind. Because I was comfortable playing in any position in the back four and central midfield, would I be typecast as a utility player, someone useful to have on the bench ready for anything rather than starting games and gaining crucial experience as a centre-back in the heat of competitive battle? All I could do was stay focused and train and play as best I could and hope that my ability and hard work would be recognized and that I would get a chance in my favoured centre-back position and I would be able to seize it.

What I didn't expect was that the problem the next season was not that I would be stuck on the bench but that I would be stuck on the treatment table. On the verge of breaking through as a regular, I would be knocked back time and again by injury.

Over the previous few seasons I'd been moving up the rankings as an England player, with four caps as an Under-16, six as an Under-17 and three as an Under-18, coached by Colin Murphy. Under Peter Taylor then Howard Wilkinson I was now being picked for the Under-21s, one of the youngest in the side. Most summers there were Under-21 games, and in one of them – I can't remember which – before the start of the new 1999/2000 domestic season, I picked up an injury.

So it wasn't until the tenth game of the new season that I played again for my club. It was away at Derby County on 16 October 1999, four days after my nineteenth birthday. It was also my first start, and I was playing in centre midfield alongside Allan Nielsen. Within ten seconds of kick-off, Derby's

Rory Delap went into me with a very hard challenge, and I knew I was in trouble. I managed to struggle through the rest of the game, but afterwards I needed an operation on my left knee to repair the torn cartilage where my knee had twisted.

Looking back, that is where the worst of my injury problems started. Not my hip, and not my feet, though I suffered with those injuries too. No, it was the knees that were to dog my career, starting that day a few seconds after three o'clock, just days after I turned nineteen years old.

Being injured is not fun, especially a long-term injury. Apart from anything else, your days are much longer than when you're playing. When you're fit and playing, you train for maybe ninety minutes or two hours a day. Generally, you'd start at ten and finish by twelve. But when you're injured, you need to get to the training ground earlier to start your treatment, then lunch and then more treatment, maybe a tea break and yet more treatment.

George Graham made the injured players stay until 4.30. As players we weren't used to such a long day and hated it. We had every incentive to get fit again as soon as possible. There wouldn't be any players faking injuries for the sake of an easy life. At times we were bored, because you would be waiting for physiotherapy. And the physios wouldn't be in any rush because they knew you weren't going anywhere. Sometimes you just walk around lost in breaks between treatment. Or just stick in your seat in the changing room.

But you didn't lose touch with your teammates, at least not back then. That's because the gym at Spurs Lodge training ground was quite small, and at the start of my career fewer players used it after being on the training pitches than do now. That meant there was room for both fit and injured players in rehab to use it at the same time, so at least you were doing something together. But all the camaraderie and banter is on the training pitch, not in the gym, so if you're injured you do start to get detached from the team.

Being in the treatment room for weeks or even months is lonely, and when finally you're fit enough to get back on the training pitch, you're like a kid, you're so happy to be back out there among your friends. You realize how much you miss them.

Five or six weeks after the knee injury in October, I returned to training. I was on the road back to match fitness and picking up my drive to become a regular first-team pick. Or so I thought. One day in training round about Christmas 1999, just days before the turn of the new millennium, I leaped. And as I pushed off I felt a click, a crunch, in my left foot. As I came down I couldn't put any weight onto it. The X-ray showed I'd fractured my metatarsal.

I was right back where I started – in the treatment room then in rehab, separated from the comradeship of the training session and the game. Once again, my playing career was on hold. Adding together the knee injury and then the metatarsal, I was out for almost the entire season.

Finally, with the season whose start I'd missed through injury almost over, I came back for a grand total of ninety-six minutes.

On 6 May 2000, just over a year after my first-team debut at Anfield, I came on again at one of the world's most famous grounds – Old Trafford. This time, with six minutes to go, me coming on as a substitute for the midfielder Matthew Etherington was not going to affect the outcome. Tottenham were 3-1 down at half-time, and George Graham's double substitution on seventy minutes of Gary Doherty and Willem Korsten for Chris Armstrong and Steffen Iversen had failed to pull the game back for us.

But things didn't get any worse when I came on for those last minutes, and I was glad to be back. And finally, a week later, on 14 May, the last day of the season, I played the full ninety minutes of a so-called 'meaningless' mid-table end-of-season game between Tottenham, lying eleventh, and Sunderland, five places above.

But that game had meaning for me. In fact it meant a lot. It was my debut at White Hart Lane.

I must admit I hardly remember the game itself. I played left-back, which was hardly my preferred position, but I really wanted to show the home fans a glimpse of what I was made of as a player. The fans have always been great to players who come through the youth team, and I really appreciate that support, because it gives you so much confidence, especially if you're a defender who is always anxious in case you make a mistake through inexperience. You've done nothing, but when your name is announced on the PA before kick-off, and you hear the cheer for a homegrown player who's come through the ranks, that's a real boost.

For some of the experienced first-team players, an end-of-season game when we were going to end up mid-table whatever happened is one with little to play for. Not for me, though. It was a big opportunity to prove myself to the home fans. Even though towards the back end of a season you sense that some of the players are already halfway off on their holidays and just want to get the season over with, for me as a young player with no wife and kids waiting for me with their passports and beach towels, that last game was massive. Even though the summer months would go by before I would have another chance to show the fans I could perform at the top level, I wasn't going to waste this one, even though it was right at the end of the season rather than what would have been ideal, the beginning.

Happily, Tottenham won 3-1. It had been a rotten season for me, but at least it ended it on a high.

It's a fact of the game that some players think that they'll be moving on in the summer, and, if they do move on, it will often be the boss's decision and not theirs. I never had that anxiety as a young player. I always felt that if I could stay fit and get a chance to play, I was confident that I could prove myself. Of course, it's hard for a young defender to nail down a position in the first team, because experience is so important in defence. That was especially so with George Graham as manager. He was very focused on defence, wanted experience and wanted his players to be men. But I had the feeling that he saw potential in me and that I would get opportunities.

When I was played as a full-back, usually on the left, I had decent legs on me so I could get forward in support of the attack. But I didn't really play overlap with David Ginola wide left because he was the kind of player you could give the ball to and he'd just *go*. He was confident enough to hold the ball and he'd only give it back to the man behind him if he absolutely needed to. So that helped me at that stage of my career.

A player in that Tottenham side at the turn of the millennium who I always got on well with was Gary Doherty, who'd arrived from Luton. 'Doc' was a year older than me, and because he could play centre-half I saw him as competition for a place. Anyone who came into the club from outside to play in defence I saw as competition, and as a homegrown player I felt I had to show who was best. Doc and I were good friends, but I never forgot I was competing with him. He was a good lad who really enjoyed himself on the pitch. Because he'd played up front, he thought he was a cultured centre-half. And because at times he thought he possessed more skill than he really had, a lot of the older players took the piss out of him – and the fans nicknamed him the Ginger Pele! But he did well for Tottenham and scored some important goals.

When he was fit, England international Darren Anderton was a player of genuine quality. He had a good engine on him for someone who'd had so many injuries. When he did play, he certainly got round the pitch. Like many of the club's senior English players at that time, Darren was quite old school. They'd treat you mean to put you in your place. A lot of the young players coming through with me were quite wary of Darren as well as of Tim Sherwood, who'd won a League champion's medal with Blackburn, and, though he was Irish rather than English, Stephen Carr. Having all played at a high level, they expected the same from you, and they'd let you know if you weren't doing something right. A bit later you realized they were like that out of love.

Though he might not have had the footballing quality of Tim Sherwood or Darren Anderton, Steffen Freund had other qualities which were an asset for whoever he played for. After all, you don't get picked to play for the German national side for nothing. He was a really nice guy but he had a fire in his belly, not only when he crossed the touchline onto the pitch but in the dressing room, when he'd really gee people up. He could break up opponents' play and give the ball to an attacking teammate, and this was just what we needed. There was no one else who could do that like him. He had so much energy getting round the pitch to break up attacks, and quite rightly the fans loved him.

So it looked as if I was finally back on track, not only making my home debut but selected after such an injury-blighted season to go to Slovakia that summer with the England squad for the 2000 UEFA European Under-21 Football Championship tournament. It should have been great. It turned into a nightmare.

I didn't know the politics of the situation, but my career as an England Under-21 had started under Peter Taylor, who'd been appointed by the national manager Glenn Hoddle – both men were ex-Spurs players, with Glenn a Tottenham legend. When Glenn Hoddle was sacked as England manager in very controversial circumstances in 1999, his Under-21 appointee Peter Taylor was also replaced despite having been incredibly successful in the job, qualifying for the 2000 tournament finals without conceding a goal. The FA's technical director, Howard Wilkinson, picked himself to take over as England Under-21 coach. After a good start under Howard, it all went wrong.

In the group stages, for which we'd qualified so successfully, we were beaten 2-0 by Italy in the first game on 27 May. But two days later we beat Turkey 6-0, and I scored my first U21 goal. In the final group game we needed to beat the hosts Slovakia in the capital, Bratislava. They had all the home support, of course, and had managed a draw against Italy as well as a win against Turkey. Despite this, we went into the game feeling pretty sure of victory.

Slovakia were a better side than we anticipated. After ninety minutes we were 2-0 down and obviously going out of the tournament. As the final whistle blew I was on the floor; I knew straight away it was my metatarsal. I couldn't put an ounce of weight on it and, as I was stretchered off, I remember thinking, here I go again – another injury. I'd broken the same metatarsal bone as I had six months before. It was 1 June 2000.

Why did I keep fracturing my metatarsal? I don't know. But I've always had flat feet. So I suppose I must put a lot of pressure on certain joints. There are plenty of flat-footed footballers around, you may be surprised to read. But maybe not with bow legs as well! So I was putting pressure on the outside of my knees and on the fourth and fifth metatarsal bones.

Flat feet and bow legs sound like deal-breakers for anyone who wants to make a career in professional football. But the thing is, I never had to pass a medical, and not just because I was never transferred to another club from Spurs. I didn't have a medical when I started as a Tottenham schoolboy trainee, nor at any stage as I rose through the ranks. The truth is that any player's medical will show up issues that can raise concerns about injury proneness. For example, a medical will show that Demba Ba has bad knees, but they don't cause him to miss any games, and he scores goals, so you judge him on that fact rather than the medical.

As for me, there was a stage when I was fine. When I first got injured, they had a look at me and corrected my flat feet with orthotics. Lots of players have orthotics to adjust imbalances. In the youth team, Ross Fitzsimons struggled with injury, and that was the first time I ever saw orthotics. You put each foot into a bucket of plaster and they take moulds from which they make orthotic in-soles for both boots.

Defeat, disappointment and last-second injury in Slovakia ruined my summer of 2000. And I couldn't even bounce back with the new domestic season. I spent the first months of the 2000/2001 season exactly where I'd spent almost all the season before: in the treatment room.

I was not yet twenty years old but already had an injury history. Would I ever get an injury-free run to show what I could do and establish myself in the first team?

IN WHICH I SET A RECORD!

Normally a fractured metatarsal will keep you out for around two months.

Not mine. Not this time.

I was out for five.

Because it was the same bone I'd broken before, the club was very careful to make sure I was fully healed before bringing me back. So I didn't play again until November of the 2000/2001 season. Before then I was on the bench for a couple of matches.

Being a sub away at Aston Villa sticks in my mind. Alton was also on the bench, and as we warmed up before kick-off we heard monkey chants from a section of the Villa crowd. We couldn't believe it. What made it even more stupid was that Villa had a leggy midfielder, Ian Taylor, and when he scored both goals against us the same section of fans cheered his name – even though he was black.

That summed up for Alton and me just how fickle those Villa fans were. Were they really racists who made an exception for their own player? Or plain ordinary idiots ready to sink to the lowest, most disgusting level just to make their opponents uncomfortable? If it was the second, it worked, because Alton and I, being young players, were hurt, and we really didn't want to have to go out there and warm up on the touchline to be ready in case we were needed to play. Alton and I didn't make a fuss. We thought it best to ignore it and said nothing to anyone, just got back in the dug-out as soon as we could and tried to put it out of our minds.

That was our first taste of racism as a footballer in this country. I'd had a taste of racism as a player abroad, and though you didn't come to expect it, you weren't that surprised either. But at home in England it really came as a shock. I'd witnessed it as a fan at Millwall a few years before, but otherwise I'd thought racist abuse of black players by English fans was a thing of the past.

The following game we were at home against Liverpool. Things weren't going well for the team. We started the day lying tenth in the table, so it was a difficult time. Because some of the senior players weren't performing as well as they should have been, George Graham decided to start two of the younger players to see if we could make a difference. When the team isn't doing that well, that will often put into the manager's mind the thought of trying different players and different partnerships. And George Graham, being George Graham, had quite a collection of defensive options to choose from.

So, replacing Ramon Vega and Ben Thatcher, Alton and I came in. It was Alton's full debut and my first game in a while, and it helped us both that the other was playing. At home against Liverpool is always a big game, and the atmosphere was amazing. The fans really got behind the team, and we felt that their support was directed in particular to us homegrown players. We felt very encouraged. I think the manager picking us lifted the fans on the day, and that lifted the team. We got a great 2-1 win.

Up against Michael Owen and Robbie Fowler, arguably the best striking partnership in the country at the time, Alton had a great debut. After the game we were both really buzzing, on a total high. Getting a home win against one of the best teams in the country was all the sweeter because I could share it with a mate who, like me, was a young player who'd come through the ranks. Together, we thought we could really push on and help the team.

I played centre midfield in that game – I was happy to be playing in any position. I liked playing in centre-mid, playing further forward than I was used to and so getting more involved in the game, but deep down I knew I was really a centre-back; that was really my strongest position. Could I have converted to a central midfielder? Maybe, if I'd trained more to play in that position. There's a lot more running around, of course, but at that age I didn't have a problem getting round the pitch.

But that season, the question for me was: what sort of centre-mid should I be? We had Steffen Freund, who was holding midfield and only holding midfield. That meant I needed to play ahead of him, linking up play box to box. But my instincts were more defensive than that. I would be quicker to see a threat to our defence than an attacking opportunity. So I was forced to be an all-round midfielder, and that was not really my strength. I was playing outside my comfort zone. I was never going to pull trees up in that position, just do the best job I could for the team. I was younger than Steffen and more expendable so had to be more flexible.

Two games after beating Liverpool we went up to Old Trafford and lost 2-0. Being on TV a lot, Manchester United's players were well known, and I knew what to expect, not that the knowledge did us much good against a side that included the Neville brothers, Scholesy, David Beckham and Roy Keane, with Dwight Yorke and ex-Spur Teddy Sheringham up front, and, coming on as supersub eighteen minutes from time, Ole Gunnar Solskjaer, who put the result beyond doubt with an eighty-fourth-minute goal.

A few games after that, just before New Year, we went up to Ipswich and got the kind of late Christmas present we really didn't want: a surprise 3-0 beating. Watching TV doesn't always prepare you for the experience of actually playing against some opponents. I thought we would dominate Ipswich because on paper we had better players. They had a midfielder called Jermaine Wright, who didn't seem to present a huge threat. But I had a really tough time against him. He was older than me and as a midfielder knew exactly what he was doing, while I was learning to play outside my best position.

Funnily enough, I'd had an easier time up at Old Trafford. Man United let you play, but Ipswich allowed you no time on the ball at all. The better teams will often let you have more time on the ball in some areas, and will wait until you get into more forward areas before they try to win it, while less good teams will chase around and try to win the ball in any part of the pitch. That doesn't always work, because really good players can get out of tight situations and expose opponents caught out of position because they've been chasing around. It's a matter of finding the right balance. Up on the big pitch at Old Trafford, Manchester United know you can't run around closing down opponents the whole time, so they have struc-tured their play to know when and where to close down and when and where to let you play. So even though I was com-peting in midfield against Roy Keane and Paul Scholes, I had more time to find a pass than in certain other games.

What I noticed was how Keane completely dictated the pace of the game, slowing things down when he wanted or picking them up again. Scholesy was all about his range of passes and was very difficult to close down because he could play one-touch and two-touch, knew when to pass the ball and when to hold it. Neither he nor Keane ever gave the ball away; they held it or passed it as they needed to and so retained posses-sion. I enjoyed playing against them, and I felt I did OK, though

I must admit that in midfield I didn't have the tools to really hurt them. And I think they sensed that.

We didn't have a great record against Manchester United, and I think they felt that, however much punishment we gave them, if they did what they needed to do, they would win. Whether upping the tempo or slowing it down, they had the quality players to dictate the game against us.

That season, the first-choice centre-backs were Sol Campbell and Chris Perry. While they stayed fit, I could see that my opportunities of breaking into the team in my favoured position were going to be few, though I was always confident that, if I kept up my progress as a player, my time would come.

Sol, of course, was quite simply one of the best centre-backs in the country, if not the world, and I was learning things from Chris Perry too. He wasn't the biggest guy, but he had a leap on him. He was nicknamed the Rash because, whether the ball was played to opposing players' feet or in front, he was all over them and didn't give them any time. He was underrated, a better defender than people knew. Even though as centre-backs we were different, I admired and respected the things he could do. But I felt that in time I had the ability to be better.

Though at that time we had some great defenders, we kept conceding goals. What often happens is that midfielders are not always in the right positions, so defenders get drawn out and gaps open up. Back then, the whole team was not defensive-minded. Everyone wanted to get forward, and not many were prepared to roll up their sleeves to do the defensive dirty work you need for clean sheets. We liked to play and not be horrible to the opposition. We were too easy to play against, not tough enough to stop goals. I think George Graham would have liked us to be that team which won 1-0, like his old Arsenal side with Seaman in goal and Adams, Bould, Winterburn and Dixon the back four. But, unfortunately for him, the team he inherited was not built around that style of play. We had players of quality but never struck the right balance between the need to score and the need to defend. We wanted to entertain without the solid foundations. And we had injuries, which meant that the manager had to change things around, so we lacked continuity. But in the end it was down to us, going out there on the pitch and not doing the right things to get the results. We needed to do much better.

Typical of our instinct to get forward is my own claim on the record books. Though never a striker, and usually a defender, I hold the record for the fastest goal ever scored in the Premiership.

It was 9 December 2000, away at Bradford City. At that time we had the starting routine where, even though I played centre-half, I took the centre. Then we played it back to a midfielder, who would hit the diagonal to the striker on the left while everybody pushed up in support.

So we started as usual, and the diag was intercepted by their right-back. As we pushed up into their half, the loose ball fell to me, I took a touch or two and had a hit. The shot took a big deflection, wrong-footed the keeper and went in, 9.7 seconds from kick-off. I honestly don't know why I shot – I was never a shooter. It was a horrible hit, and when it went in I was very surprised and a bit embarrassed, as you can see on the TV footage, where all my teammates are celebrating more than me. At the time I realized it was quick, and though I didn't think about it at the time, I see now that the record will be hard to beat.

As for the rest of the game, we got to a 3-1 lead then threw it away for a draw. Typical Tottenham, or at least typical of the side we were at the time.

When George Graham was sacked by the club four months later in March 2001, it was not a total surprise. With his affiliation to Arsenal, the fans had never taken to him. And the team wasn't really performing. But he had given me my chance as a young player, so I was sad and disappointed. The senior players, I think, felt differently and were looking forward to working under a new manager. That they felt like this may be a clue as to why the team had not been performing to its fullest potential. Later on, I was to see again how some players might subconsciously give less than their best efforts when they no longer believed in the manager. On top of the substandard performance level and results on the pitch that season, obviously the club felt he wasn't the right man to take us forward in the future.

Taking over as caretaker manager for the time it took to appoint a new permanent manager, the club's director of football and former manager David Pleat was someone you'd see around. He was always nice to me whenever I bumped into him.

I know people have speculated all sorts of things about the politics of the situation with him as ex-manager still at the club as director of football, but I was too young to concern myself with any of that. The older players would discuss managers, but not me. The subject never came up when I was around. I just focused on coming in and training and playing as well as I could. The older players would certainly want to know who's coming in and might even have been involved in the appointment process, but I knew I could never affect that decision so just concentrated on playing as well as I could to try to prove myself to the new manager, whoever it was.

In this case it was the Tottenham legend, former manager of Swindon and Chelsea, then England coach Glenn Hoddle. In total contrast to George Graham with his Arsenal associations and old-school emphasis on hard-working defence, Glenn was Spurs through and through, one of the world's great playmaking midfielders in his '80s heyday and progressive, even visionary, in his coaching style. It cost Tottenham a lot to wrest him from his job as Southampton manager.

I'd never met Glenn Hoddle before he became manager, though I'd obviously seen him on TV as a player late in his career with Chelsea and Swindon and really admired him. I was excited to work with someone who'd been such a good player, and his number two, John Gorman, was a lively character. I knew that a manager couldn't really know how good a player was until he worked with him every day, I couldn't wait to show them both in training what I could do.

Sunday, 8 April was Glenn's first game in charge, and it was the FA Cup semi-final at Old Trafford against Arsenal. It was a lovely sunny day, and the Spurs support completely outsang the Arsenal fans. Whatever the balance of power between the Spurs and Arsenal teams, between the two sets of fans there has only been one winner for passion and the boost they give the players.

I was on the bench, the first time I'd not been started for months apart from the immediately preceding League game, again against Arsenal at Highbury, due to pulling a muscle. So being on the bench at Old Trafford when I was fit to start disappointed me. I think Glenn Hoddle was looking for solid match experience in this crunch game when we were just ninety minutes away from our first FA Cup final in a decade. And when the Doc scored his third goal of the season's FA Cup campaign, the new manager's selection seemed vindicated against such a powerful Arsenal side.

But Arsenal pressure began to tell, and in a tussle with Arsenal's Ray Parlour, Sol injured his ankle and limped off the pitch for treatment. While he was on the sideline, Pirès lofted a free kick for Vieira to score with a header.

I came on for Sol after thirty-eight minutes and immediately had to pick up the pace of the game. Before I'd really got my legs going, the ball dropped by me and Ljungberg just burst past me onto it, and I thought: wow. We'd started well and hoped we could hang on and nick the game and so get into the final. But Arsenal were the fitter side with better athletes, and we were playing on the big Old Trafford pitch. It was not to be, as Arsenal ran out 2-1 winners after a Pirès goal on seventy-three minutes. With the FA Cup final chance gone, it was the first time in sixty years that Tottenham would end a season in a year ending with a one without a major trophy.

Six days later we were trying to put our disappointment behind us away at Sunderland. Kevin Kilbane and I both went for the same ball in the air. I got there first and a fraction of a second later his head went into the side of mine. I was knocked out for a second or two and came to on the side line, but said I was OK to come back on. I was too dazed to realize that I wasn't. Back on the pitch, I remember looking up at the scoreboard and it said 2-0 to Sunderland, and wondering how we were 2-0 down already; I asked one of the other players. But we were 2-0 down when I was knocked out – I just couldn't remember it. The next ball that came to me I dealt with, but gingerly, still in a bit of a daze. Stephen Carr saw I was in trouble and signalled to the bench to get me off.

I went to hospital and was diagnosed with a fractured cheekbone. I didn't want to stay overnight in Sunderland so far from home, so I returned with the team on the coach, sitting there very quietly with my face swollen and throbbing, and didn't sleep too well that night. Later in London I had an operation where they went into the side of my head between my ear and cheekbone and lifted the bone. I was used to knee and ankle injuries so a facial injury was new to me. No operation is fun, but when they're going into your head, that was not something I was looking forward to. I was a little bit wary, to say the least.

Over the summer I made a full recovery and was looking forward to starting the new season and a new era at Tottenham under Glenn Hoddle. But that July an earthquake shook White Hart Lane, one that would undermine the foundations of what Glenn Hoddle was trying to build even before he'd started, rock the world of English football, traumatize Spurs fans and set off aftershocks that rumbled on for years afterwards. But it was one that would create a vacancy at the club for a home grown defender who would represent the stability, loyalty and pride in the club that the fans craved. Not that I thought of any of this at the time. But in hindsight, what happened in July 2001, more than any other event, gave me the chance I'd been looking for.

THE DAWN OF THE HODDLE ERA

Sol Campbell was always a quite a mysterious character who kept his cards close to his chest. He didn't confide in us or share information freely. He didn't talk too much but when he did, people listened. We knew he was strong-minded and thoughtful. So when he spoke, we knew he'd put a lot of thought into what he was going to say. But he said nothing to us, the players alongside him in defence, who he'd taken a small interest in thanks to our shared East End background, during all the months that speculation grew about his future over the course of the 2000/2001 season.

Sol Campbell was the leader of the team and our best player. With his contract running down, he had obviously spent the season considering his future and looking at what was out there to better himself as a player. We all knew that it didn't look as if he would sign a new contract with the club. That uncertainty about your best player and leader committing to the team made it difficult for both the other players and the manager, George Graham, who lost his job before the season was out.

I think that uncertainty may have affected Sol's performances too, though he always tried his hardest.

While I think some of the players suspected he would leave Tottenham at the end of the season when his contract came to an end, I don't think any of us had a clue where he'd be going next. He was without question one of the finest central defenders in Europe. Inter Milan, Barcelona, Bayern Munich and Manchester United were all linked with him – huge clubs in the Champions League, where he wanted to be, offering massive wages, as they would sign him for free on a Bosman deal with his Tottenham contract having elapsed.

But Sol was saying nothing, hinting nothing.

To be honest, I thought he might even sign a new contract and stay at Spurs; that's certainly what I hoped. But I didn't know what offers he'd had or what was in his head. I don't think any of us did.

So when it was announced he was going to Arsenal, I was as surprised as anyone. I could see the attraction of Arsenal, because at that time they seemed to have it all: the manager and the players who would have been a dream for anyone to play with. Except they were a no-go area for Tottenham, the players and fans. Anyone but that team, is how the fans saw it. I know the fans felt betrayed that our star player who had come through the system had gone to our rivals, and they had a right to have their say.

Sol was not easily swayed and he did what he thought was

best for him and his career. He made his choice. I could never have done what he did, but everyone's different, and nothing surprises me now in this world.

My view then and now was that Tottenham were not falling behind in ambition. Bringing in Glenn Hoddle as manager showed that. To replace the experience we'd lost in defence, after months of acrimonious negotiations with his old club, Southampton, he signed Dean Richards for over £8 million, a record for an non-international player.

Dean had almost the perfect debut for Tottenham, scoring within fifteen minutes at home against Manchester United on 29 September 2001. By half-time we were 3-0 ahead. What could possibly go wrong . . . ? Manchester United had a great team, including Beckham, Butt, Keane, Van Nistelrooy, Andy Cole, Gary Neville and their new signing, the Argentine international Juan Sebastian Verón. But we were up for it and came charging out of the blocks on fire, buoyed by our own new signing, Dean Richards, and the atmosphere from the fans was electric. A new player can often lift his teammates and the crowd. After Dean had scored the first goal, Les Ferdinand made it 2-0 on twenty-five minutes, and then, just before half-time, German international Christian Ziege, who'd replaced David Ginola on the left side of midfield that summer, made it 3-0. It was a dream come true.

But, going in at half-time, we didn't feel the game was over. And the manager obviously didn't feel we were home and dry either. We sensed a little bit of fear back in the dressing room. Hoddle's whole team talk was about not conceding early in the second half. I think that scared us, and we went back out there on a negative note. Sure enough, just one minute into the second half, Andy Cole pulled one back. At that moment everyone sensed what was going to happen. Collapse. What *should* have happened is that we should have remembered we still had a fantastic 3-1 lead, and just needed to get our heads right. But our heads were scrambled and stayed scrambled. We panicked.

Sometimes half-time can really change a game. Some sides really need it. But in that game we didn't need or want it – we wanted to play ninety minutes straight through. But Man United really changed things around at half-time. Having already brought on Solskjaer for Nicky Butt, they then brought on Mikaël Silvestre for Denis Irwin, and were very attacking. The whole second half was wave after wave of attack, growing in confidence as they sensed we were on the ropes. Slowly but surely they picked us off, beating us 5-3. What should have been a great game for us turned into a nightmare. It was a bitter pill to take.

Worse still, it's a game people talk about and show to this day. I get sick and tired of seeing it on ESPN Classics.

Back around then there was paper talk that Leeds were offering Spurs £10 million for me to play alongside Rio Ferdinand. I remember the manager saying they wouldn't sell me for £30 million. The respect the manager had for me as a player gave me confidence that I was going along the right path. And a few years later there was a sniff from Mourinho at Chelsea. But I was enjoying my football right where I was at Tottenham, and the thought of going anywhere else never crossed my mind.

As I was trying to improve myself; I wanted to take the team with me in the right direction. We were a mid-table team, and I wanted us to be fighting at the top end. I had that feeling because I'd come up through the youth system so totally identified with the club, and I know that Stephen Carr, who'd also come up that way, felt similarly, but he got a serious injury and was never quite the same player again. But players who'd been bought from other clubs didn't always have quite the same sense of commitment to Tottenham.

And then there was the homegrown player who'd so controversially lost his commitment to the club.

On 17 November 2001, Sol Campbell came back to White Hart Lane for the first time as an Arsenal player. That was a match to remember. Any time you play Arsenal the game is a bit different, as the atmosphere builds up during the week. But this week there was not only the normal anticipation of the derby but the fact it was Sol's first time back. The fans you met and the newspapers gave us all a sense of the game building up, and by the time it came around, you knew how big it was going to be.

You also knew that it was going to be hell for Sol, and that he was going to get it. But I don't think Sol was prepared for the level of hate, and as Spurs players we were shocked too by the intensity throughout the game. But, as this was a huge game against our fiercest rivals, we were going to try to use that red-hot atmosphere to our advantage, even though it was directed at Sol personally. We were going to feed off the energy from the fans and gain strength from it, and hope that all that hatred affected the performance of the player for whom it was intended. For me personally it was my chance to prove that Sol wasn't missed too badly on the pitch, to prove that his leaving hadn't also left a big gap in defence.

That was the game when I think I first heard the chant from the fans, 'We've got Ledley at the back.' And that was a little bit of extra pressure on me rather than him, because I had to back up that faith in me with a performance on the pitch. It ended up a draw, and I think I played well, and so did Sol – he didn't appear too rattled in that game. But when the hate kept coming every time he returned to White Hart Lane with Arsenal, I think in some games it really got to him, and you could see from his performances that it did affect him.

But whether that hatred might have put off any other Spurs player from even thinking about going to Arsenal, at that time not many of us would have interested Arsenal. Secondly, that level of hate would only have been reached again if another homegrown player went there – me! And I certainly never thought of going to Arsenal. I might have had friends who played for Arsenal but I wouldn't have gone to play for them myself if they were the last team on earth.

Of all the strikers in the Premier League, I think Thierry Henry was the biggest challenge to contain. You could have a really good game against him, yet he'd still have that quality in reserve to pull off something special. He drifted around so much between the wings and coming inside; that's tough to stop, and that elusive movement is what made him special. Playing against him, your right-back, right-midfielder and right-sided centre-back needed to have a very clear under-standing between them of how they were going to stop the ball getting to him. If the right-mid can't block the entry pass to Henry, then what does he do? Does he come inside? Follow? These are the things you needed to have discussed and pre-pared yourself for in training.

When Glenn came in as manager the training routine changed dramatically. I loved it. Hoddle was a flair player, and his sessions were very technical, with lots of balls to encourage the team to play. Later on he even broke with England's 4-4-2 tradition and had us play with wing-backs and three centre-backs: Dean in the middle, me to the left and, to the right, Chris Perry or Goran Bunjevčević or Gary Doherty or Anthony Gardner, who suffered from injuries and so found it hard to nail down a regular position. Glenn wanted us to be able to play out of defence and get forward. He wanted me as a left-sided centre-half to enjoy the freedom of getting forward, and sometimes I ended up on the opposite byline. That's the kind of freedom that we had.

Glenn liked the formation with three in midfield; with the wingbacks, he felt that the game could be won in midfield. I liked playing in that 5-3-2 or 3-5-2 formation, which was a bit of a rarity, and at that age it suited me. It gave you options. Nowadays managers want players to be able to adapt to playing in different formations, but there wasn't too much of that when I was younger.

In training we would play a lot of small-sided games, and both Glenn and John Gorman would get involved. Hoddle was still a great player with his touch and passing, doing things which made me wish I'd seen him in his prime as a player. He looked as if he could still have played with us in the first team. John didn't have the same technique but would put himself about, and the players would give him grief when he gave the ball away. He was full of energy, and that's what you need in your number two: someone who comes in and keeps up the players' spirits. There was a good spirit at the dawn of the Hoddle era.

Teddy Sheringham had come back to Spurs after winning everything at Manchester United, and I'd seen his quality for years back as a fan of Millwall and then on TV with Forest, Spurs and United. The fact he was coming back was great for me because it showed the club was attracting a winner. His enthusiasm for the game, and his keenness to practise techniques after training with me and Simon Davies, had a great effect on our careers. The fans loved Teddy, and he was the captain. His career lasted so long because his appetite for playing and training was so great. He was very competitive, even when he was relaxing. After training he'd play golf, and on the coach to and from matches he'd organize the card games. PlayStations and Game Boys were getting popular with the younger players who'd grown up with computer games, but old-school footballers like Teddy preferred old-school games.

When I first came into the senior team, cards were played on the coach, and even though I hadn't grown up with cards, I wanted to play to try to fit in. Chris Armstrong, Stephen Clemence and, if I remember right, Luke Young played this game called kalooki, and they always needed me as an extra body to make up the four. It's also called Jamaican rummy because it's popular on the island where my family came from, but I'd never heard of it before. I hadn't a clue how to play so I had to learn it from scratch. There were so many cards to hold I couldn't believe it. My cards were falling out of my hands all over the place, so Chris Armstrong called me Ledley Scissorhands. I was only playing to be one of the boys and I didn't really know what I was doing, so my money was just going down by the week. By the day! I was pretty pleased when the older players moved on and cards went out of the window!

Of other big personalities at Spurs at that time, Stephen Carr had fire in his belly from a young age. Tim Sherwood was another leader, as was Steffen, and Les had character on and off the pitch. And alongside Dean Richards and Teddy, Glenn Hoddle brought in Gustavo Poyet from Chelsea, so there was no shortage of experience on the pitch. These were older players, and as a younger player you accept the situation and stay focused to move forward.

The players that I was friendly with were in my age group – Alton Thelwell, Gary Doherty and, getting more first-team games, Anthony Gardner, bought by George Graham from Port Vale. These were the guys I was training with now and sitting with on coaches to away games, the guys I hung around with on and off the pitch.

Around my age but different as characters, so I had a bit less in common with them, were Simon Davies and Matthew Etherington. They had arrived from Peterborough and were playing around the squad; these two young players Teddy took under his wing, because they had more in common with the older players and tended to mix with them more – they liked golf and playing cards. But they were good lads who worked hard in training, were easy to get along with and were made to feel welcome. They'd played in the first team for Peterborough so understood what playing in any first team was all about, at that time more than I did, even though I had, in my fewer first-team games, played at the top level with full internationals and superstars.

With all those new players of my age getting into the first team, for me it was like a new beginning.

So there were two age groups in the first team at that time, with Teddy's very experienced generation at one end and mine at the other, and not many players in between. But we all mixed, and there was a good spirit. As a younger player you're pleased to have a contract and aren't thinking too much about the future. And of course you're used to players coming and going. Obviously, when you become an older player, you think a lot more about what your options are for the future. But I was still very focused on getting on with my development as a player, very quiet, keeping my head down.

I was like that outside club duty too. People always wonder how footballers spend their time after training, which usually finishes at around twelve. Some of the older players were into golf and playing cards, but with me, it was all about resting. I would go home, lie on the bed and relax, often having a sleep. Every now and then in the evening I'd get up and go and meet my friends who I grew up with, Emerson and Stephen, and we'd go and play pool. I had a very simple lifestyle, because that's what I liked. I was never into anything glamorous.

Around then, at the age of twenty-one, I moved out of my mum's. I wanted to live in an area familiar to me in East London so I bought a flat in Wapping by the river, near Darren Anderton and Steffen Iversen, though I didn't know that when I made my choice. Buying nearby at the same time was my friend Ashley from Arsenal; we had the same agent. Football agents do a lot more than negotiate contracts. Good agents and management companies understand that they need to provide a wide range of services and expertise to help their clients to get on with the job of playing. Our agents have different experts in different fields to help the players. They introduced me to my accountant, Melvyn Gandz, and my property and financial adviser, Patrick Deane. I've known these guys throughout my professional career, and Patrick would come out looking at places with me, giving me the benefit of his expert knowledge. Without all these guys around me with their knowledge, advice and help, I would have struggled to stay focused on my football.

The next thing was to pass my driving test. You're on your own there. I'd been taking driving lessons since I was eighteen, but not very many, about ten of them. I wanted a car but I didn't like all the bother you have to go through – like lessons! – so was taking my time about it. My instructor was Chris Hughton's brother-in-law, Andrew. Over the years he'd taught several of the young players and knew how to make them comfortable. He'd pick me up straight from training, which was good, because I didn't have to make my own way back home first. Once I was in his instructor's Nissan Micra car with him, and someone recognized me and shouted, 'Oi, Ledley!' and burst out laughing to see me squeezed into such a small car. That set my driving lessons back a little!

The driving test was one of the most nerve-racking days of my life. My foot was shaking uncontrollably, and as we were going upstairs in the test centre Andrew said to me that they might test my eyes, so told me to look through the window and read out to him the numberplate of a car he pointed out. When I came back down again with the woman giving me the test, she stopped at the same window and told me to read out the numberplate of the same car! I was so nervous I was getting all my numbers and letters jumbled up, and the nerves continued in the car. I stalled a few times, and at the end of it all I was convinced that it was a 100 per cent fail. Amazingly, I passed first time.

I was so pleased, because now I could go to work without having to get lifts from other players, and I bought a Mercedes C-class. I was playing regularly in the first team now, so my money had gone up, and I felt I'd better drive something appropriate. It wasn't mega-expensive, but it was certainly nicer than most people's first car.

So for me personally as well as for Tottenham, it was looking as if 2002 would be a very good year. But hiding just around the corner were lows as well as highs.

CAPPED – AND HOODOOED

The 2002 World Cup finals were split between Japan and South Korea. England had topped the qualifying group the previous October thanks to David Beckham's last-gasp equalizer against Greece, but in the finals that summer found ourselves having to break out of the so-called 'Group of Death', which contained Sweden, Nigeria and our old adversaries, Argentina.

Just a few months before, in February, I got my first call-up to the senior team. Rio Ferdinand and Sol Campbell were fixtures in central defence, but you never know what might happen between the end of the season and the summer. Even with the Far East World Cup admittedly a long shot, you can imagine how thrilled and honoured I was to be called up for what would have been my first senior cap – a friendly against Holland. Darius Vassell, Wayne Bridge and Michael Ricketts also got the call, so I was relieved I wouldn't be the only new kid on the block in the England camp.

The manager was Sven-Göran Eriksson, a very nice, quiet, laid-back guy. His assistant, Steve McClaren, took most of the training sessions while Eriksson stood and watched, very calm, and didn't say too much. I think he was looking at one or two players he could maybe sneak in the back door, just in case.

When we got to Holland I started to feel really rough. Whether it was flu or food poisoning I don't know, but I was knocked out and couldn't get out of bed. The squad went to the game, and I was so sick I didn't even watch it on TV. My mum had flown out to watch me too! And after the game – a 1-1 draw, with Gareth Southgate rather than me coming on for Sol, whose mistake had led to their goal – the squad came back to the hotel, picked me up, and then we flew home. So that was a disappointment.

But I only had another five weeks to wait before my chance came again to make my senior England debut, which came in another warm-up friendly, this time against Italy, on 27 March 2002, at Elland Road. We changed teams virtually at half-time. I came on in the second half and played all right, even testing their keeper, Buffon. We did well, better than the first-half team I think, but lost to a stoppage-time penalty.

As I knew deep down, the World Cup in Japan and Korea would come a bit too soon for me. By the time I did manage to get my first cap it was a bit too late. Sven had made his selection. But he needed to be looking ahead, beyond 2002, and I was still only twenty-one, young for a central defender, a position where experience counts for so much. I didn't feel that I'd had my one and only chance – far from it.

Just as I was getting my first senior cap, I was also in the hunt for silverware for my club. I'd been too young to be part of the 1998/99 victorious League Cup campaign, but in season 2001/2002 I made my debut in the competition in a win over Torquay, and the run continued past Tranmere, Fulham and a 6-0 thrashing of Bolton. But then in the semis we were drawn against Chelsea.

Our record wasn't good against Chelsea. In fact, when we went to Stamford Bridge for the first leg, Spurs hadn't beaten the West Londoners in twelve years and twenty-five games. But it was too early in my career for me to feel personally they had the Indian sign on us: I didn't feel that weight of history dragging me down. I never thought we were beaten before we started.

But at Stamford Bridge it seemed to be the same old story when we lost the first leg 2-1, their winner coming from a free kick by Jimmy Floyd Hasselbaink after the ref awarded a hand ball against me. But with our away goal and just one to make up to bring the tie back to terms, we felt we had a chance back at the Lane.

We were under no illusions of what we were up against, though. Chelsea had good attacking players. Scorer of both goals in the first leg, the big, powerful striker Jimmy Floyd Hasselbaink liked to play off the last defender, and the smaller, nimbler and more skilful Gianfranco Zola could find spaces and drop into holes. When their manager, Claudio Ranieri, chose not to play Zola, his younger replacement, Eiður

Guðjohnsen, was a lethal predator. When defending against strikers who could play off each other so well, communication between us was key.

I watched players on TV, of course, and I knew who were the fast strikers. But once on the pitch I never felt anyone's pace caused me a problem; nor I was ever stripped. If I knew someone might be faster than me, I tried to make sure I was never in a position where that would count against me, and fortunately, on a football pitch rather than on a running track, there was never too much in it. You can slide, which you can't do on the track.

I always wondered how strikers thought through the same issue from the opposite viewpoint: if you knew a defender was fast, wouldn't you pick a slower defender to spin off his shoulder? If you were good in the air, wouldn't you sooner attach yourself to the shorter defender with less of a leap than a tall one who could spring? I'm sure they must try to make those choices, but to get into scoring positions they must move to where the ball moves, whoever's trailing them.

So back to that Wednesday night in January at White Hart Lane, where we hadn't beaten Chelsea since 1987, when I was six years old! I'd been rested in the previous League game against Everton and came on fresh and feeling sure we had it all to play for. Les had been concussed in that Everton game, so Steffen Iversen stepped in for his first match since the start of the season.

In front of our fans, we had one of those magical nights when everything goes right. We got out of the blocks fast, and from the first minute to the last they couldn't live with us. Almost every time we went forward we scored a goal, picking them off goal by goal. Though they could claim that Hasselbaink was wrongly sent off, many others said that it was, in fact, Mario Melchiot who had pushed Teddy in the face. By then we were 3-0 up, and the Blues were on the run. The crowd was electric, and that gave us energy and self-belief. We did everything right, and it was one of those games that felt easy.

Yet a few weeks after that, Chelsea got their revenge in the FA Cup sixth round, beating us 4-0 at the Lane, and by the same scoreline just four days later at Stamford Bridge in the League. We had no consistency. Yet when we got it right, you could see what we could do against a top side like Chelsea.

Where the same sides could play each other within weeks and get such different scores, did luck play a part? Yes and no. Players believe in luck – sort of. I had my good-luck routines and superstitions. Lots of players have them. I'm told that John Terry counts lampposts on the way to the stadium; a pity he didn't lose count on the way to White Hart Lane more often.

With me, if we won a game, I would repeat the same pre-match meal and the one I'd had the night before, and have the same snack, like a banana, and the same drink, for the following games until we lost, when those meals had clearly stopped working. I'd often wear the same trainers and the same pants

– making sure they were clean! – and would try to remember what boot I put on first, and what top I wore in the warm-up and whether I had gloves on, and I would try to repeat those things too.

But there is a method to all this. When we won I usually had played well, so I would do the things that seemed to help me play well, and these would change. Back when I used to take the centre at kick-off, I would jump twice in the air before the whistle. The one thing I always did from my first to my last game would be to stub my toe on the touchline as I crossed it from the tunnel or bench onto the pitch. It was my sign to myself that this was the battleground and it was time to go to work.

So we got to the final of the League Cup – back then called the Worthington Cup after the sponsors – at the Millennium Stadium in Cardiff, home to English football's showcase games while Wembley was being rebuilt. It had opened for business less than three years before but already had a history: of the two team changing rooms, the north was lucky and south was unlucky. Something like the last ten beaten finalists in a cup or promotion play-off had been assigned the south changing room. The stadium management had even commissioned a feng shui expert to carry out a blessing and an artist to paint a mural to try to defeat the 'bad spirits' cursing the room, but so far nothing had worked. The hoodoo continued to jinx every team assigned to that changing room. Spurs were assigned the notorious south changing room.

We'd read the papers and were aware of all the talk leading up to the final; we'd heard about the unlucky changing room and we knew that it was the one we'd been given. But you try to brush that unlucky toss of the coin aside and not let that sort of thing get into your head. And I firmly believe that luck didn't play any part in the game itself. We didn't lose because we got the unlucky changing room; we lost because of the kind of team we were back then. And unfortunately that game summed us up. We went into the game as favourites, especially with our run to get there and record in cup finals over the years. But we didn't dominate as we should have done. We felt the game was ours to lose rather than a game to go out and win. We didn't set out with any winning urgency.

Blackburn were a dogged side. We would have been better off playing a team against whom we would have been the underdog. This was our downfall – the sides we were supposed to beat made it hard work for us, made it a scrap. It was a big pitch and though we tried to get the ball on the floor to play, Blackburn made it very hard. And for all Tottenham's internationals, Blackburn also had quality players, like Damien Duff and Matt Jansen.

Losing the game was my biggest disappointment. It was my first final, and I'd started the game full of confidence, so defeat was a very bitter pill to swallow. Especially the fact that it was my mistake that gave away Blackburn's winning second goal.

The score was 1-1, and we were pressing for the second goal;

we felt that if anyone was going to win the game it was us. Blackburn hit a long, high ball into the box, which I was stretching to head. I just got it, and it bounced away five yards to head level again, like a dropped ball. I thought I wouldn't be able to get any distance on it with a header to clear it out of danger, so I took a little touch with my head to get it down to where I could volley it out. Closing in, Jansen stuck a foot out and touched it into the path of Andy Cole, who, of course, being a top finisher, scored. It felt like harsh punishment, because it was a nothing situation and yet a goal resulted from it – a weak goal, too.

Going into the last minutes 2-1 down, we were chasing, really going for it, and I was pushed into midfield to create chances. Les Ferdinand had almost scored with a header from a cross, and then Iversen headed from point-blank range – in my mind's eye I saw the net bulge and I feel a surge of relief that I'd got away with it. But their keeper Brad Friedel saved, and had a brilliant game to keep us out. They say that when you're chasing the game with five or ten minutes to go, you only get one chance – and that was our chance.

We kept plugging away, but it was not our day, and the goal didn't come. Years later, Brad joined Spurs, and the player who basically won the game for the opposition in my first final watched my back just as brilliantly, though by then he was over forty years old.

Of all the Spurs players, I think I was hurt the most by that result. I didn't say a word after the game all the way home. I felt like a broken man. There were other times when we lost and I felt I hadn't played well and would get very down, but this felt different. I'd actually played well on the day, but then my mistake cost the team so much, and I took it badly.

I couldn't stand to be reminded of anything about the game. I didn't want to read anything, watch anything or hear anything. The manager did say afterwards I should have headed it away or done something different. I was the never the kind of player to do nothing with the ball, and thinking back, to this day I would have done the same thing. Rather than nod it down for a volley, could I have headed the ball five yards ahead once it had popped up in front of me with my second header? Yes, but had I headed it five yards, which was the most I could have done at that stretch, it would have gone into no man's land for anyone to pick up, so that wasn't dealing with the problem. On a football pitch you're put into tricky situations, and sometimes you get caught and punished, and that day I got punished.

That game shook me up. Of course, when you're young, in defence you won't always have got into the best positions and seen things as early as you should, and in the course of a season you will have been part of a defence that conceded goals. But you hope that in the next game you can do something about it with a performance that helps your teammates collect three points. But when, in a final, a one-off, a winner-takes-all game, it's you who has made the glaring error which loses it for your teammates, you have no opportunity to redeem yourself.

For me, still aged twenty-one, what happened was more than a knock to my confidence. It was a crisis. Was my judgement all wrong? I seriously asked myself if I should still play the way I wanted to, playing the ball out of trouble rather than just hoofing it, though I've always known when that has to be done.

I became so anxious about making mistakes after my decision had cost us so big. Before then, the game had felt natural to me; I played on instinct with the skills I'd acquired over the years without consciously thinking about it. But afterwards I started to worry and overthink every situation in case I lost the ball and once again conceded a goal. I started putting unnecessary pressure on myself and making things twice as hard. And over the next few games I was wary and nervous.

But over time I got my confidence back. It is true what they say: what doesn't break you makes you stronger.

After losing that final we badly wanted to make it up to the fans, and we beat Sunderland at home. But then we were battered badly by Man United and Chelsea, both of them quality teams going for high League position and, in Chelsea's case, also wanting revenge for our 5-1 semi-final win. Not having anything to go for, we made it easy for them.

We finished the season ninth, an improvement of three places on the season before, which in turn was two places below what we'd achieved the season before that. In short, we looked to be stuck as a mid-table side. Daniel Levy had taken over from Sir Alan Sugar as Tottenham Hotspur's chairman the year before, and we knew he was ambitious for the club. Mid-table wasn't good enough. The next season had to see real improvement.

LOSING THE FAITH

There were games around that time when we had a flurry of red cards. Mauricio Taricco and Gustavo Poyet, both fiery South Americans, would be most likely to get sent off. Poyet always had an aggressive streak; you could see that's how he was brought up. Even during training in small-sided games he'd get the hump when his teammates were running around like headless chickens, and he felt it was not good enough. Occasionally in actual games the fire in his belly would work against him when, trying to lift the players around him and show some grit, he'd leave his foot in and get into trouble. There can be a thin line between getting the team to react and follow you and leaving the team with only ten men.

Taricco was the same: a very underrated player, calm, assured, understood his position, would never kick the ball out of play under pressure. He could be facing the corner flag, a position no defender enjoys being in, with a man breathing down his neck and his back to the play, but he always had a coolness that meant as soon as he felt a touch of pressure from an overzealous forward, he'd go to ground and win us free kicks. I used to wonder how he got away with it every time – to me, it didn't often look like a foul. That's the South American style: you get your body between your opponent and the ball, and any contact is a foul. It's a great skill to have, and not enough players know how to protect the ball with their body. It shows how composed Taricco was on the ball; he wasn't one for knocking it out of play to concede a throw and give away possession. He won so many free kicks from that position, turning defence into attack.

I've seen Taricco have plenty of battles over the years when he and a winger could go at it, and I've seen him leave a winger in a heap. And yes, in March 2002 he was sent off, twice in two games, against Manchester United then Chelsea, both games we lost 4-0. Like Poyet, Taricco didn't like it when we as a team were made to look stupid, and if he wasn't happy he would leave his mark. He was a gritty player at a time when we didn't have enough of them.

Though Glenn Hoddle was under pressure to improve on our mid-table status, over the summer of 2002 he only brought in one new player to refresh the squad. But he was a good one: Robbie Keane.

Robbie had caught my eye as an opponent when he played for Leeds. He's my age, and I remember thinking how great his movement was for someone so young and who wasn't a Continental or South American player; he was better than most strikers I'd come up against. British forwards tended to be a bit static and move on predictable tramlines, but Robbie would come short and spin behind, or go behind then come short; he was a tricky customer. He could play as striker or just behind, and he could finish too. When he joined Tottenham, seeing him train day in day out confirmed how good he was.

Robbie was a great character, really bubbly, not shy or in awe of any of the older players but never in a bad, disrespectful way. He was Irish too, so Stephen Carr took him under his wing, but Robbie felt at home and at ease straight away. That was his nature, and he'd have been just the same if he hadn't been a footballer. He was a quality player with a huge love for football and was a great signing for the club.

Meanwhile I was back in the treatment room. Back in May I'd had to withdraw from the England Under-21 squad for the European Championship in Switzerland thanks to a niggle, and then, before the start of the 2002/2003 season, a hip problem kept me out for the first thirteen games.

I came back into a side where performances and results were no more consistent than they had been the season before. From January it got worse. Tottenham had been knocked out of the League Cup back in November, and in the third round of the FA Cup we were hammered by Southampton, the club Glenn had left to manage Spurs, 4-0. We picked ourselves up to win the next two League games, but then lost eight out of the remaining fourteen, the last two drubbings from Middlesbrough and Blackburn.

Something had gone wrong. But what?

The problem was Glenn Hoddle, or at least the way some of the biggest players at the club had lost faith in his management style.

It's been said that some of Glenn's training methods went over players' heads. I don't think they did, and certainly not mine, but Glenn did have a different way of thinking. Whether genius or not, he saw things differently. I remember once a player had some kind of injury and he placed his hand on the leg or foot as if he were a faith healer; it looked to me as if he were trying to channel the power of the will to make it better again. He had on his coaching staff a guy he'd had at Southampton, John Syer. We called him John the Head because that was his job: to get into the players' heads and help us visualize winning. We'd have meetings where we'd sit together and pass a pen around to each other like it was a microphone, closing our eyes and visualizing what we wanted to do on the pitch the next day and telling everyone all about it. For young players it was a little bit daunting going and sitting in a room with all the team, and having to speak about your feelings on the pitch. It wasn't something that I particularly enjoyed, but I'm up for trying everything, and if it works for one or two people then it's a success.

So I didn't have a problem with his training methods, because when you're young you're more open-minded. But you could tell that some of the older players didn't have any time for that technique. It's not for everyone. I don't think you can force everyone to try everything, but the ones who want to do it will take it upon themselves to try. Everyone felt embarrassed. No one really wanted to say, 'You know what? Yes, I enjoy this; it works for me.' I think a few people may have kept it quiet and had their own little individual meetings with John. It's about getting the best out of the individual.

John the Head was around the place a lot. I felt sorry for him because he was an older man, and you could see that he was passionate about what he did, but the players didn't really share his passion. A few of them felt John wasn't really a football person and didn't show him too much respect. It was a tough time for him.

So, some of the senior players just didn't buy into Glenn's training and motivational methods, especially when he brought in meditation and visualization. The older players didn't want to listen. They had their own way of doing things and didn't want to be forced to think about it or do things differently.

But the problem between Glenn and some of the senior players ran deeper.

Glenn used to train with the lads and even at his age then, well past forty, you could see what a talent he was. He had that confidence about him when he was on the football pitch, that arrogance you need to be one of the top players. And I don't think you lose that. He was like a magician. Just imagine what he was like playing back in his day. I think it's quite normal that, when a player becomes a manager, you remember what you could do on the pitch yourself and want your players to be able to simulate that talent, like your puppets, your mini-mes.

For any player who had been as talented as Glenn, it must be hard as a manager to see your players unable to do the things you used to be able to do. Things he would try to teach would sometimes be not as easy to the players as they were to him. I could see how that could be demotivating to the player who could see he just didn't have the ball skills of his manager. That's where you need to be a good man manager and under-stand how to deal with different players. But some of the senior players didn't feel that this was Glenn's strength. They didn't find him easy to talk to or get along with. And I think they felt that in his mind he was still the star of the show and that he loved himself too much. These were things that just didn't sit right with them, and they lost respect for the manager.

I've never been managed by anyone I didn't basically respect, so I can't imagine what it must feel like for a player who lacks that respect, and whether subconsciously that lack of respect for the manager can turn into lack of effort on the pitch. On the pitch you expect that everyone gives 100 per cent all the time, and I felt that everyone was still giving 100 per cent whether they got on with Glenn or not. But we had a lot of older legs out there, and not a lot of grit. We were a flair team. We could do damage when we had the ball, but we weren't very good at stopping teams. When it worked, it worked well; when it didn't, we struggled.

I was aware of some discontent amongst the older players. For instance, when he left the club in the January 2003 transfer window after a row with Glenn, Tim Sherwood went on record as saying: 'No one at Tottenham would shed a single tear if Glenn Hoddle was sacked tomorrow. The dressing room is not together, and there is no team spirit. He has absolutely no man-management skills.' He was speaking for himself and maybe some of the other old guard, but certainly not for me and perhaps some of the other younger players.

I've heard since that a few of the older players actually went to the board and told them they weren't happy with the manager. But at that time I had no idea. Back then all that stuff didn't bother me. I was there to concentrate on my football. I think other players sometimes paid too much attention to what was going on and not enough concentrating on their own game.

Glenn lasted just six games into the start of the following season. His last game as manager was a 3-1 home defeat by his old club, Southampton, whose away support enjoyed their revenge for his deserting them for big-city Spurs. It was our fourth defeat so far out of six games that season, and we had four points out of a potential eighteen. Not even legends are fireproof when the results carried on where they'd left off at the end of the previous season: bad.

When Glenn Hoddle and John Gorman were sacked, I felt for them. But our chairman, Daniel Levy, was and is very ambitious and wants the club to be successful, and as soon as possible. He'd given Glenn that summer of 2003 to rebalance the first team with new players and get them back into winning ways after the losing run at the end of the previous season. But it didn't work. So, to put it mildly, when he made his decision with the home defeat to Southampton, the chairman didn't see an adequate level of success under Glenn and was not persuaded by his vision of how far the team could go under his management.

As with the departure of George Graham before, it was the end of another era for Tottenham that had started with high hopes but ended in disappointment. For me, I learned a lot under the contrasting management and coaching styles of both men, and I am grateful to them for their encouragement, the opportunities they gave me, and the ways they helped me develop my game and improve as a player.

And I felt that, as long as I could come back as soon as possible from the injuries I was beginning to pick up with increasing frequency, I had everything to look forward to from whoever took over next at the top of Tottenham Hotspur.

PLEAT TAKES CARE

At the start of the 2003/2004 season I was still only twenty-two, but those injuries weren't going away.

Prior to the Southampton game, I did a hamstring before half-time against Chelsea (another side Glenn Hoddle had managed) when we lost 4-2 at Stamford Bridge and was out for six weeks.

When I came back, firstly as a sub in a goalless home draw against Middlesbrough, I found myself playing in a team using a flat back four for the first time in ages – but in front of them as a central midfielder. Under Glenn Hoddle, I'd played in a back three with two wing-backs. After Glenn left, when David Pleat had a spell in charge as caretaker, we reverted to a flat back four, and I was converted to a holding midfielder, because that was where the squad was weak. During the summer Glenn had bought three strikers – Hélder Postiga, Freddie Kanouté and Bobby Zamora – but no one to replace the grit in midfield of Steffen Freund and Gus Poyet, who had both moved on.

Even though the club now had more choices as striker,

playing a rigid 4-4-2 formation, we found it harder to create chances than under Glenn's 5-3-2 with wing-backs.

David Pleat reacted to the previous manager's advanced training methods by stripping it right back to basics. To be fair, David Pleat tried to make training fun with things like shadow-boxing in the warm-up and players on each other's backs. While new kids Stephen Kelly, Johnnie Jackson and I had all come through the youth team and were used to his training methods, some of the foreign players who'd signed to the club felt they were too old school. They just didn't get it.

Part of the problem we had that season was that the players knew that David Pleat was the caretaker manager and would not be around the next season. Knowing that did not reinforce his authority, even though, despite not knowing what the club's longer-term strategy might be, you still took it a game at a time and tried to win that game, not looking too far ahead. Answering the question of whether you'll still be at the club the following season, you want to play well whatever, because you're playing for your future, wherever it might lie.

But was the team under David Pleat happier than under Glenn Hoddle? Under Glenn it was never unhappy, even though in any team you will have players who don't always take to the manager. But those older, stronger, senior players – Tim, Darren, Les, Teddy – had now left the club. Under Pleaty the squad was younger, with experienced players like Jamie Redknapp brought in to help the team.

Some new players came in at the time. Jermain Defoe, Michael Brown, Freddy Kanouté and, from the youth team, Johnnie Jackson. With Jermain, Robbie Keane and me, we had young players but with proven ability and first-team experience that you could see moving forward in the following seasons.

Kasey Keller was in goal. A nice and intelligent guy who I got on well with, Kasey was over thirty when he joined Tottenham. Like a lot of Americans, he had a wide range of interests other than football, and he loved his music. To be honest I couldn't really class what he loved as music because it was so heavy – it was the heaviest stuff I've ever heard. He tried to get me into the moshpit a few times – he loved to throw himself around in the moshpit and let off steam, a different animal with his hardcore buddies than the guy we knew on the training ground and pitch. So yes, in his way, a classic crazy keeper!

One player who rocked up on loan from Inter Milan broke the golden rule of footballers, which says that you can be anything you like as long as you do the business on the pitch and are not a horrible person. Stéphane Dalmat did the business on the pitch, all right: a box of tricks who could open up things for us. But he was not popular in the camp; he was widely regarded as a rotten egg. He didn't speak or understand English, so maybe that made him paranoid that players were saying bad things about him. But there was none of that. We had several foreign players, and there wasn't that kind of atmosphere of us against them.

Dalmat seemed so angry all the time, as if he thought all his teammates were against him, and he was pissing a lot of people off in training. If he didn't like a tackle, it would almost come to blows. Tempers can get heated in training, but some of his confrontations with coaches and other players completely overstepped the mark. I lost count of the number of times he walked off the training pitch. Pleat would tell him he was out of order and send him inside, but the next day he'd be back in training again, and we just had to accept that he was talented and could do things on the pitch we needed because we were really struggling.

The fans could see how talented he was and really appreciated him, but I don't think many of them knew what he was like as a personality. The rest of the team kept our feelings about him hidden in public because we needed him to be playing well. But in the end we just couldn't keep training with him acting the way he did, and Pleat sent him back. Though I could see he wasn't a pleasant player and not easy to get along with, I never had a problem with him personally. In my career, that was as wild as it got.

We had good players but I don't think we had the most talented of teams as judged over the duration of my career. When we believed in ourselves as a team we could win games, but our problem was inconsistency. We could win two games then lose two. We seldom hit a winning run, or, to be fair, a long losing one either. One run we did go on was a goal frenzy, both for and against. Against Manchester City, Portsmouth, Charlton and Leicester in February 2004, each game averaged seven goals.

Jermain Defoe scored on his debut against Portsmouth in that run and then again and again over the rest of that season. His signing worked straight away. Jermain played two years below me at Senrab, so I hadn't seen him play when we were kids, but I knew he was a goalscorer and a poacher from his progress through Charlton and West Ham. I was delighted that he'd come to Tottenham.

He's a very bubbly character who thrives on being the centre of attention on the pitch and in training. He's different to me in that respect, but we had a lot in common in the areas where we grew up, schools, people we know, so from day one we had plenty to talk about and got on well.

Jermain has his Christian beliefs but doesn't thrust them upon other people. Being religious is not that unusual among footballers at the top level. And in football we have a live-and-let-live attitude; people can be who they want to be, and we respect each other's beliefs. Some players were Muslims; for instance, Freddie Kanouté would get his mat out in hotel rooms before a game and pray, and a few seasons later Zokora would as well, and put on his robe, which we all had a bit of fun with.

Everyone has different characters, and as long as you do the business on the pitch, no one has any problems.

When we signed him, I could see that Jermain could form a good striking relationship with Kanouté. And we had Keane as well, who could play as a striker up top, the old centre-forward position, or behind. Scoring goals, we had options. Conceding them was the problem. We had to score four or five just to be sure of winning a game. The defenders weren't enjoying conceding so many, nor was I, the holding mid who had played in defence. You can win a game 5-4, but the defenders won't have enjoyed it as much as the fans. Clearly, something was not right in defence. Of the back four, injury meant that it was seldom settled. Unsettled as we were, we lacked concentration, and that would cost us.

Of those four consecutive games back in February 2004 which yielded twenty-eight goals, the one that everyone remembers – Tottenham fans for the wrong reasons – was the FA Cup fourth round game at home against Manchester City. It was a replay after a draw up at Eastlands, when Gary Doherty scored a late equalizer. Coming back to our place, we felt we had a great chance of going through to the next round. At White Hart Lane I was in midfield and scored quite early on, probably the best of my career: I ran into the box on the right side, feinted to go outside but cut in and whipped it into the top corner with my left foot from twenty yards. Our two other goals that half were also of real quality: Robbie Keane got a ball from Stephen Carr over the top, his control was instant, with a great first touch, and he just dinked it over the keeper. Then Christian Ziege scored a good free kick, and at 3-0 up we were buzzing.

And it got even better for us. At the half-time whistle, Manchester City's Joey Barton stepped over the mark talking to the referee and got his second yellow, sent off as we were walking down the tunnel. We were delighted, as the game had just got even easier.

So what went wrong? To this day, I don't really know. But I think a big part of it was we didn't have a game plan for the second half. Yes, of course, with nothing to lose in a cup-tie Man City would go for it. But we also knew that, if you're 3-0 down in the first half, it's for a reason, and that if you go into all-out attack to try to get back into the game, you risk being picked off for a 6-0 drubbing. Even though in a cup game goal difference doesn't matter, a drubbing can still knock the confidence of players for their next League game. But if you know that by doing nothing you're out of the cup anyway, you might as well go for it – to a sensible extent, where you cut your losses if your attacks expose you to conceding further goals. That was certainly the attitude of Man City's manager, Kevin Keegan, who always believed in attack, but not suicidal attack.

Slowly, slowly, Man City came back, putting pressure on us, and got one goal back. With that goal, their belief grew.

From our viewpoint, when their first goal went in, we felt comfortable; when their second went in, we still felt comfortable. When the third one went in, we didn't believe it – but we still see didn't ourselves losing the game. But they were taking their chances, and the momentum had shifted to them, and they believed they could now win the game. We still didn't think that was possible, but by now we were embarrassed that with ten men they'd pulled the score level. I was playing by then at left-back, and they put in a cross from the left which went over my head for Jon Macken to head down into the goal for their fourth, the winner.

The City players went mad, the City fans in the corner went mad. We were in shock. We wanted the pitch to swallow us up. It was a game we wanted to forget as soon as possible. It was not a good day, not a good day at all.

That season we took a late-season fortnight's break in Dubai. Though we still trained in that heat, it was about letting our hair down and bonding as a team. Which we did. But when we got back from that trip it was mayhem. Until the very last two games of the season, we couldn't buy a win. The team spirit was great, but the results were not. Many people thought the problem was that going away broke our concentration. But before we went away, the fact is that we had nothing to play for, and when we got back that was still the case. We'd recharged our batteries but not found a new purpose or direction; the season still felt over already. Without something to go for, I think a lot of players' minds were still away on their break.

We had the talent but not the steel. Tottenham was seen as a nice club: nice to play for, everything about the club was nice. I think opposition clubs liked playing at White Hart Lane because it was a nice game of football. We wanted to entertain, not clog and scrap and do whatever it took to get the win. We gave our opponents time and space, which led to open, entertaining games, but games we would often lose in front of our own fans. The heritage of the Glory Game was our problem; we wanted to entertain at all costs, even if that cost was defeat. This was unlike Manchester United, where the message to the players and staff from the manager was clear and consistent: you come here to win, and on the pitch and off, at all times, you represent the biggest club in the world. A club which knows how to entertain, but above all how to win.

Could Tottenham find the formula to get us back to playing the winning style of the Glory Game?

A CAPTAIN IN STORMY WATERS

For two years, from the time of Glenn Hoddle's departure, there was a lot of change at Tottenham. During David Pleat's caretakership, behind the scenes the club completely rethought the structure of football management to something more along the lines you saw at the time on the Continent, where the functions of the manager were split between different people.

After the 2004 Euros, which had been cut short for me by my personal emergency, Jacques Santini's name was being touted at Tottenham as manager. That sounded OK to me. He'd been coach of France, a great side with top players and big names, so to recruit him as coach showed that Tottenham had real ambition. I was relieved that back in June I'd had a decent game against France, which gave me a head start over some of the other players who Santini didn't know at all.

It was a whirlwind time. There were other new people around, but obviously Santini was the big appointment, coming from the France national team to take the Tottenham job. At this stage we players felt we had a good squad but were up for something new. The new challenge was a foreign manager.

When Santini came in, he changed quite a bit in training. He was very technical in his approach, walking us through the shape of the team and how it might change over the course of the game. That approach was just what we needed. We needed guidance on tactics. We'd never had that kind of help before, and I think that had held us back. We were a talented bunch of players who should have done better but until that point hadn't the game plan.

With neither Santini nor his assistant Dominique Cuperly speaking great English, at the start of their time at Spurs a lot of preparation on the pitch got lost in translation, so we had to work hard to understand what was being demonstrated. A key lesson was what to do when we didn't have the ball. That is a very underrated part of the game. Santini encouraged us to get our opponents, when they were in possession, to channel the ball in a certain direction with our positioning and body shapes. He also explained where the ball needed to be before we should start pressing.

That kind of instruction made things a lot easier. Beforehand, we didn't really know whether to press or not when we didn't have the ball, and that indecision would lead to hesitation, breakdown in formation and an awful lot of energy-wasting chasing the ball. As players we react to given situations, and one thing will trigger another. If we all know what we're doing and what our teammates will do, it makes things a lot easier.

By then I was the longest-serving Tottenham player, and

Santini gave me the captaincy. It was a big deal for me. I felt like I was growing up and maturing.

I was lucky enough to have a great role model as Tottenham captain – Jamie Redknapp. I'd first met him a few years before he joined Tottenham from Liverpool, when both the England Under-21s and the senior players were returning from playing overseas. Back then, the two teams would be on the same flight, the seniors up the front of the plane, us Under-21s at the back. But he made a point of coming back to sit next to me for a chat. I was eighteen then, so it was great for me to sit down with a top England international who was also a top player at a top club, which Liverpool very much were back then. Jamie told me that he'd seen me play and what a good footballer I was. That meant a great deal to me, and when Jamie signed for Tottenham three years later, I reminded him of the time when I was eighteen, and he was nice to me.

Jamie's not just a top bloke but a class player too. I was delighted when a player of such great experience and quality came to Spurs under Glenn Hoddle. It's just unfortunate that with his knee injuries he only got to play forty-nine games in less than three seasons with us. At Tottenham you could see his quality both on the pitch and in training; he could pass with both feet and jink both ways, and he wanted the ball and was brave on the ball. It was sad that he couldn't fulfil his full potential at Spurs before the injuries took their toll.

I always enjoyed Jamie being at the club and looked up to

him and tried to learn from him. And when I was appointed captain after him, I tried to follow his example. You always try to be yourself – you don't want to be fake – but you learn little things along the way from different people and how they manage certain situations. It's not just about when to step in and when not to on the pitch, but about recognizing those times when you might have to speak out to the manager when it's not in your nature but because you know you're saying the right thing on behalf of the team or an individual player. If so-and-so's not happy, you have to be the go-between. As you go along things happen, and you talk and you find ways to deal with it.

Captaincy was new to me, but as the season developed I found myself enjoying it. No longer in midfield now that we had Pedro Mendes, Michael Brown and Sean Davis, I'd settled into my position as a centre-back in a back four. I felt comfortable and I was finding my voice on the pitch, becoming more authoritative.

I wouldn't often try to regulate the tempo or intensity, because that's hard for a defender to do. Those commands need to come from midfield. I saw my job as keeping the players on their toes and getting them going. Back then, it was not the captain's sole responsibility to speak to the referee on behalf of any of your teammates; it was still a free-for-all, with the Man Uniteds of this world crowding the referee and disputing decisions. But it was your job to calm things down when things got heated. Ours was a pretty even-tempered team, with fewer players who would lose their heads compared to earlier in my career, but occasionally I needed to have a word with Michael Brown, who was older and more experienced than me but liked to put his foot in, and I had to tell him to calm down. He would live on the edge with his tackles and yellow cards. Then there was the Cameroonian Timothée Atouba, a good lad and a bit of a character, certainly not nasty or malicious. He was someone I felt I needed to keep on top of, more to snap him out of dips in concentration than anything else.

The first few games of the season started off pretty well, beginning with Liverpool at home, always a tough first game of the season, and we deserved to win rather than concede a goal from Djibril Cissé on his debut, with Jermain Defoe scoring the equalizer. It was Rafa Benitez's first game as Liverpool's manager as well as Santini's first at Tottenham, and our new manager also picked five new players including a really promising left-back who'd come through the youth system called Philip Ifil. He was seventeen, played brilliantly for three or four games and then dropped out of sight. He was someone I used to talk to quite a lot and try to help with his game; he loved to talk and wanted to know what was going on, interested in everything. I sensed he really wanted to become a top professional footballer. But he struggled with injuries and fluctuating weight, and I wonder whether he had too many distractions going on in his head. He was a good lad and a promising player, and I'm sad that he didn't progress.

At the other end of the age and experience scale but new to White Hart Lane, an overseas centre-back from whom I learned quite a bit was Noureddine Naybet. He came to Tottenham at the start of the 2004/2005 season aged thirty-four, so probably past his best. I knew that he'd been a good player for Deportivo de La Coruña but until I played with him I didn't realize how good he was.

He stepped straight into the side and we were playing without really knowing him. It was all a bit of a rush to learn about each other's style and get used to him. He could hardly speak a word of English, either. Our styles were totally different and it took me a while to understand his way of thinking and playing the game.

I was still only twenty-three so had good legs and trusted myself in a race. But at his age he preferred to play the offside trap by stepping up past the opposing striker before the forward ball was played. For that to work, the entire back four needs to coordinate so that no other defender plays the striker onside by not stepping up too. But there were occasions when he would step up and I would drop back towards our goal to read the danger and cover the striker's run, and we got ourselves into a few awkward situations. The following season, at Charlton, Darren Bent scored two goals that way. Benty's whole game was based on hanging off the last defender and waiting for the through ball or ball over the top played from Danny Murphy. By then Naybet was only four months away from turning thirty-six, so you can appreciate why he'd sooner try to play the offside trap than take on Benty in a foot race.

My view then and now is that, unless you're in real danger, there's no point in taking the chance that the offside trap will work. If it doesn't, or the referee's assistant doesn't judge it right, then you can get into real trouble. You can be too clever. But I do understand what Naybet was trying to do. To get it right, it's about communication and knowing each other, understanding each other. I would have to be aware that he would get caught on the ball from time to time, and also out of position – sometimes a long way out of position, thanks to his attacking instincts. I would occasionally be played as a left-back, and when we went on an attack down the left, I would check behind me to make sure everything was all right at the back, and often Naybet had gone missing. He would bomb up the middle to get into the opposition box and join in the attack – at the age of thirty-four he was fit enough to do that. This was how he was brought up as a player, his style, and he wasn't going to change for anybody. If we lost possession, he'd be well out of position, and we'd be in trouble.

The first time I saw him do this came as a shock. In England we were taught as defenders not to get forward unless you were bringing the ball out or, like an overlapping full-back, supporting an attack down the wing. I had to mop up around him.

But I liked his style and freedom of play. When you can express yourself to the fullest and do as you please as a footballer, you get the best out of yourself.

The pairing of a very experienced centre-back and a younger partner with better legs can work very well. I suspect that Naybet was composed and assured throughout his playing career and not just as an older player. When I got to know what his game was about, he taught me things which really benefited me, especially when I began to get more injuries later on. Then, as a player who didn't really want to run, I remembered how he played as a footballer who also didn't really want to run.

Another new boy at Tottenham was Timothée Atouba, who used to worry us because he was so relaxed and confident as a player with the ball that he'd try to take players on in our own box. But the next game that season, away at Newcastle, he scored a brilliant goal which won it for us.

Then we went to Chelsea and played really defensively to get a point from a goalless draw. Before the game their manager José Mourinho had said that we could beat Chelsea. But, as Joe Cole told me much later on, that was only a ruse to get us to open up; he had his way of saying things to try to get at other teams. There is a lot of thinking behind everything Mourinho does. We were known for coming to play football, and Mourinho knew that too, I think. But that Chelsea side were stronger and better than us, so circumstances dictated that, if we wanted any points out of that game we had to defend in depth. They had the ball and kept pushing us back, and we had to stand up to that.

I didn't care one bit when Mourinho complained afterwards that we'd 'parked the bus' rather than let Chelsea score against us. We were not a team known for being able to grind out nil-nils away against top-four opposition, and I was pleased that we were now up for the scrap rather than rolling over. For me it was great because I was now playing in an organized back four, and I was starting to see the team grow up a little bit. To keep a clean sheet against the likes of Drogba was a boost. So nil-nil was a result for us and represented progress away from a losing mentality against top opposition, and we were delighted.

But there were things going on behind the scenes that were undermining what to us looked like progress. Also starting with Santini and his assistant Dominique Cuperly as a coach at the club but not part of the same package was Martin Jol, who'd been coach at RKC Waalwijk in the Dutch League; he'd played for West Brom and Coventry, spoke excellent English and had a lot of experience of the game in this country. I think he'd been selected for these reasons to complement Santini and Cuperly, neither of whom spoke much English, by Tottenham's sporting director, Frank Arnesen, who'd also come in the summer as part of the club's strategy of adopting the Continental model of dividing the traditional football management functions of coaching, man-management and playing and technical staff recruitment between different specialists.

Frank Arnesen's office was in the training ground, so you would see him. I didn't really know too much about him apart from realizing that he was a talented player in his own right. He used to speak about his fellow Danes, the Laudrup brothers, who I recognized as great players. I got on quite well with Frank. We used to chat a bit, and I think he recognized my talent. But again I wasn't too sure what was going on behind the scenes in terms of Frank. I didn't really pay too much attention to what was going on off the field.

When Martin Jol was first brought in, no one really knew too much about him. But from really early on you could see there was a conflict in styles between him and Jacques Santini. I don't think Martin and the French coaches had the same ideas at all. I'm not sure how much they really spoke to each other, and they were definitely not on the same page in their methods and their tactics. Often we would find that Santini was telling us one thing and Martin Jol was taking us to the side, speaking to players individually and telling us not to do that. We were getting mixed messages, being told one thing by one coach and the opposite by the other, who would tell off the player for doing what the other coach had trained him to do. I'm pretty sure there were times when players were confused on the pitch because they'd been told two different things by two different people.

At the time we thought, there are some new players here, we've got new coaches, a completely new structure and system, so we've got to give it time to settle down. And the season didn't start too badly: draw at home to Liverpool, beat Newcastle away, draw West Ham, beat Burnley, draw Norwich, draw Chelsea, lose at home to Man U, beat Everton away. Then we hit a bad run: lose to Portsmouth, beaten at home by Bolton, beaten by Fulham and beaten by Chelsea.

Losing at home to Bolton was all the worse because that morning the death was announced of the great Bill Nicholson, manager of the legendary double-winning side, the first of the twentieth century; and Bill was also the first manager to win a European trophy for a British club. As the rain poured down, the flags flew at half-mast at White Hart Lane as players, staff and fans stood in silent tribute and then, when the minute elapsed, everyone clapped long and loud in memory of the glory the great man brought to the club. We knew we had a lot to live up to, and we didn't seem to be getting very close.

As the results deteriorated, the tensions behind the scenes must have come to a head. I think Jacques Santini felt undermined. It was an awkward position for everyone, because they all sincerely held their coaching beliefs, so there was no reason why they should pretend to have different ones just for the sake of harmony.

I don't think that's the only reason why Jacques Santini left in November after only thirteen games. I think he got a bit homesick. He was quite a strange character, quiet, and he never looked too happy.

In the end, Martin Jol wanted to be the manager. You could sense that Martin wanted the team for himself, wanted to take control. He seemed confident about his knowledge of the game and could communicate better than Santini so probably felt he could manage the team better too. But it was still a surprise when he actually got the job. I don't think the players saw that coming.

It was 5 November, Fireworks Night, on the evening before the home game against Charlton. Santini had introduced a new routine before home games: after Friday-morning training at Spurs Lodge, we'd go home and do our own thing that afternoon then drive to the stadium, leave our cars there, jump on the coach and travel twenty minutes up the A10 for an overnight stay in the Marriott Hotel in Cheshunt in Hertfordshire. I think some players were quite pleased to be away from home before a home game, to get a peaceful night's sleep in a hotel. I can't say it was something that I particularly enjoyed; I like to be at home in my own bed to sleep, especially before a home game. But you deal with it. Or at least get used to it.

Anyway, around six in the evening we got to the stadium, and someone said there's a meeting going on. Any time players were called for a grand meeting it would be strange. You know that something's up so you fear the worst. There was a bit of tension in the air as we all made our way to the changing room.

You could hear a few whispers that the manager was going to quit. In the changing room it seemed like we waited for hours but it was probably just five or ten minutes. Santini came in and he looked sad, and perhaps a bit embarrassed. In his broken English, he said that he was going to be leaving. It came as a bit of a shock, and especially the night before a game it wasn't ideal. But you could tell that he was an emotional type of guy, and I think everything had just got on top of him, and he'd decided enough is enough.

Once we'd made our way out of the changing rooms, Santini and Dominique Cuperly were in the corridor, and Dominique was crying his eyes out. I'm not sure when this decision was made, but that night Dominique was very cut up about it. He didn't speak much English but he was very passionate about his job, quite army-like in his approach to the fitness side of things. But you knew he was a good guy, and it was sad seeing him in tears.

But this is football, and we had a game the next day, so no real time to reflect. We had to pick ourselves up. Martin took charge of the team, but at no point that weekend did we suspect that he'd be stepping into the manager's shoes on a permanent basis.

The game itself seems like a bit of a blur to me now, which we lost 3-2, after being 3-0 down on fifty minutes. I think we were still in shock in the first half and not focusing.

That evening Martin told the media he wanted the manager's job, and at Monday lunchtime Frank Arnesen announced he'd got it.

With no fanfare, and in the middle of an early-season crisis, a new era began at the club. We had no time to form expectations. We had a League Cup away game against Burnley the following evening, with the North London derby at home on the Saturday. Martin had thrown himself and us in at the deep end. Would we swim or drown?

ENTER THE LION!

Not many people remember us beating Burnley away 3-0 in the League Cup, even though it was a great start to Martin Jol's official tenure as manager and a huge relief and confidence boost to everyone after such a bad run of results.

But everybody who was there or watched the TV highlights remembers the North London derby four days later at White Hart Lane.

Quite often against Arsenal we'd come out all guns blazing and start really well. And that day we started well when Naybet popped up unmarked at the far post to get on the end of a great Carrick free kick to put us 1-0 up. Even with all their great attacking players on the pitch – Henry, Bergkamp, Ljungberg and Reyes, with Pirès and Van Persie on the bench – we felt fairly comfortable against anyone, especially at home. We thought that, if we really go at it, we can win. And with that one-goal lead, we were having a good go. But just before half-time Thierry Henry got a goal back for Arsenal with that bit of magic he could produce, slipping between me and Naybet to poke it home. We'd had him under control for forty-five minutes, but you couldn't lose your focus for a microsecond when he was around, and we did.

Just like that, the game was one-all going in at half-time, so we felt a little bit hard done by. But we still believed that we were in the game; we still believed that we could win.

But it got worse, with the next two goals we conceded the consequence of silly defensive errors by good players losing the plot: Noé Pamarot gave away a silly penalty, and then, in no danger, Naybet fluffed the ball, presenting it to Patrick Vieira, who bombed forward to score.

But for individual quality, the highlight of the game came two minutes later when Jermain slalomed through the Arsenal defence and unleashed an unbelievable diagonal shot into the top corner with no backlift; that amazing goal completely silenced the Arsenal away fans. The secret of his shooting power with no backlift is the combination of very strong legs with little feet that are just perfect for making contact with the football. Some players' feet are too big to make clean contact, but his are just right. He can hit the ball where he wants to.

Yes, the second half was the crazy half. They scored, we scored, they scored . . . it was a basketball match. It was one of those games where sense flew out of the window – and I've played in a few of them – with players in the heat of the moment and intensity of the game doing things they wouldn't normally do. It just becomes a free-for-all. Like Ljungberg's goal from a great Fàbregas reverse pass in the area: how did we fail to clear the ball and allow them to get so close?

Every time they thought they'd done enough, we kept coming back. I scored our third goal when we were 4-2 down; another great Carrick diagonal free kick arrived at pace into their area, and I outjumped three of their players to head home, making it 4-3 to them. But Pirès scored their fifth, and then, just as the clock was ticking towards an Arsenal victory by two goals, it was their turn to blunder – Thierry Henry, of all people, giving the ball to our Swedish left-back, Erik Edman, who laid it on for Freddie Kanouté to score in the eighty-eighth minute.

We kept on coming but ran out of time. We didn't have enough in the end but we give it all we had. When you play the basketball game against the likes of that Arsenal side, you're not going to come out on top too often. They had a bit too much quality.

So it ended 5-4 to Arsenal. We came up short again, which was disappointing. But fans still talk about that game. It was a great game to watch for a neutral. Me, I hated it. Never mind how many goals we scored, we conceded five! We could have won 8-5, and I still would have hated it.

But there was some encouragement to be drawn from that game. Arsenal had a strong team with great players, and we recognized that they were ahead of us. But on our day we knew that we had good enough players to compete with and hurt them, and if we played well we could beat almost anyone.

Most of the players liked Martin, and I certainly enjoyed my time under him. Once he was manager we started to see his real personality. You could see there was a real love for the team. Martin was a big, strong, powerful guy, and he wanted his players to stand up and fight for everything. He didn't want them to get bullied out there on the pitch, as no manager does. He wanted his players to be men.

In meetings Martin would tell stories about when he was playing and he'd often talk about being a lion. Once he asked a few of the players the question of who from the team would they take if they were going to war or were in a fight. A few players said this player or that other player. And he said, 'You should take me – I'm a lion!' He made it clear he could look after himself. So you know he had that kind of animal instinct about him. But he wanted team togetherness too – he wanted us to be lions and fight for each other. We liked that about him, that passion that he had.

But he liked intelligent players too, later on buying Tom Huddlestone and Dimitar Berbatov because they were football-intelligent. In Martin's first season, football intelligence is the reason he liked Michael Carrick so much.

Michael Carrick had come to the club from West Ham, who at that time had a great generation of young players they were forced to sell. When he came to Tottenham, Carrick was unbelievable. He had such poise in the midfield and played so high on the ball. As a defender I like players you can give the ball to even when they've got someone behind putting pressure on them because they're comfortable enough to receive it and make the right decision, whether to give it back to you or find a pass. I love midfield players like that. Some managers will say giving the player the ball when he's running back towards you is a bad ball. But to me it's not a bad ball if you've got a player who knows what he's doing; he will just give it back to you, and then it's your decision whether to play the next ball into the space he's created behind him because the opposing midfield players have come with him – space where you maybe can find your front man. Or if he doesn't play the ball back to you, a very good midfield player will take a touch on it because he's that confident and he will hold off his player and then pick the right pass. Carrick was brilliant at that. His distribution and playing the ball into the front were brilliant too; he could play balls round corners and he does it to this day. He's a really underrated player.

Much flashier but flickering rather than shining consistently in his two years with the club, another player who stood out in the second half of that 2004/2005 season was the Egyptian Mido. He came in on long-term loan from Roma, and after only a couple of training sessions he was chucked into his first game, against Portsmouth. We were behind but got back into the game and won it; that was the lion-hearted spirit of the team then – we felt like we could get results away from home. Mido scored two great goals, and I felt, yes, we've got a player on our hands here. I remember watching him train back then, finishing on his own after the session was over; he would do a volley and one would fly into the top corner, then another would fly a mile over. But he had a left foot; you could see that he had ability. He would try the unpredictable.

He got on well with the players and kept the lads amused – a good character to have around. He was well-spoken with good English, and you could see that he'd been to many different countries and was confident in his ability. He was strong-minded as well; he'd been around, he was mature for his age. We couldn't believe that he was the age that he said he was – just turning twenty-two when he arrived at Tottenham.

But something was missing, something wasn't quite right. He seemed to have problems with his weight. He came back one pre-season and he'd slimmed right down; he was skinny now and half the player, so to speak. It's strange, but some players perform better when they're a little bit heavy. But mostly the problem was that I think he was a bit of a playboy. He had a reputation, and I think he'd fallen out with a few managers. But we were a team who wanted to get to the next level, and if we felt that any player coming in could help the team do that, we were all for it. So, a talented player, a nice lad as well, and very passionate, but at times a bit too opinionated, and he would clash with Martin Jol. I think they had a liking for each other, so though they clashed at times it would be all forgotten about; both of them brushed it off. Even when he was on loan, you could see that part of his personality. He was that type of character, one of those guys that you'd have a clash with, and you never really took it personally.

After Mido's loan period at Tottenham, Martin signed him, so the club still felt that there was something there to work with. But it was a bit of a case of once he'd signed he didn't really do it; when he was on loan he was hungry and he had to prove his worth. Sometimes subconsciously players come off the boil a little bit. It was sad he didn't manage to get the most out of his career because he had ability.

On the other hand, in the January 2005 transfer window, Martin bought two players in a deal from Nottingham Forest, one of whom, Michael Dawson, has been a lion for Tottenham ever since. Three years younger than me, when Michael joined he was a young boy but he'd played a good few games at Forest so was fairly experienced. He was easy to play alongside because you knew exactly what you got from him. He wasn't one of those young defenders where you're not sure what they're going to do positionally and you have to keep an eye out in case they're in the wrong place. Dawson wasn't like that; he was a mature centre-half and he liked to defend the proper way. So I didn't really see myself as having the job to mentor him.

I always thought he was a good partner for me. He likes to put his head in there and is great in the air. He's better with his feet than people give him credit for as well – he can play from the back. He complemented me well: he used to go in there and battle while I used to try and pick up the bits and cover him. I've always admired him and always enjoyed playing alongside him. We definitely formed a good partnership.

Now he was solely in charge, Martin Jol changed our training and tactics entirely round to his way of thinking. He advocated 'splitting' at the back when our goalkeeper had the ball to give him two outlets – left or right. We tried to push the left full-back up the left wing while the left centre-half would then really spread out to the left side; the right-back would be on the right and so on, opening up the pitch. It's the keeper's judgement whether he plays it or not. Many times you see a keeper looking to make the kick or throw out wide into attack but he doesn't feel safe to do it, so he tells everyone to get their shape back and get up the pitch.

Martin also wanted the midfield player deep to pick up the ball from the keeper. He liked the players to play the ball forward early. He liked to get the ball out wide. He loved the wingers on the ball. If you could get the wingers in a one-on-one situation, that was his dream. Whenever a player was in the middle he was always shouting, 'Get out wide, get out wide.'

Though Martin loved getting the ball out wide, we didn't at that point have the players to really cause the damage that he loved in wide positions. In the deal which also brought in Michael Dawson, the wide player Andy Reid arrived from Nottingham Forest. When I say 'wide' player, I think he was naturally a heavy kid, but in training he was like George Best. He would do amazing things in training, score great goals. But on the pitch at Tottenham for some reason he just couldn't do it; for some reason it didn't work out. He used to run out of steam, which wasn't great, but I think he was one of those players who, if he lost weight, wouldn't have been as effective as he was.

With Andy's form blowing hot and cold, he was not the player who Martin had hoped he would be. The search for the wide player who would complete his tactical vision of attack from the flanks would have to continue into the summer's transfer market.

Despite taking over the reins of management in a crisis, Martin did well to get us to ninth in the League at the end of that season. The team spirit was great, in players like Michael Carrick, Jermain Defoe and Robbie Keane we had real quality, and under Martin we looked forward to making real strides the following season.

Personally, things were good for me too. Apart from the captaincy, I'd had an injury-free season, playing in every game.

I was also a new dad, of course. No longer living in a flat in Wapping, I now had a family home in Crews Hill, just outside Enfield. And if the baby sometimes got me up at night, he more or less allowed me to stick to my routine of an afternoon kip, something I felt was best for my performance. So I was happy in my family life, happy in my football, everything was fine. The new season could not come quickly enough.

THE ROAD TO LASAGNE-GATE

This season after the Euros I'd come back a new dad, a proven international and feeling like a new man confidence-wise. I'd become the captain of the team and I managed to play every League game that season. I was really feeling good about myself and the team moving forward. What's more, we even started the season with a trophy, having overcome quality opposition like Real Sociedad, Boca Juniors and, in the final, Lyon, to win the showcase Peace Cup in South Korea. So we came out of that pre-season tournament feeling good about ourselves. It gave us confidence going into the season that we could have a good one.

Personally, having played all thirty-eight League games the previous season, like anyone I had my niggles. But I was basically fine. I'd had a good few years when my knee wasn't really a problem. The next season, though, my knee and other problems started to creep in, and I'd often miss a training session.

The problem started in that pre-season. As I recall, we were doing some kind of running for a bleep test, where, in order to test your cardiovascular system, they time short sprints you make triggered by hearing bleeps, and I didn't really want to do it because I felt something bothering me. I think the manager wanted me to go and do the run, so I did. After the bleep test we were going down to do some football work, and walking from the bleep test to the pitch I think I kicked a ball, made some kind of little movement you wouldn't think twice about, and something went; I think it was my hamstring.

So I missed the first four games of the season. But aside from a home defeat to Chelsea (yes, the bogey team seemed to be back in full force), we were looking good. For his first full season, Martin had strengthened the side in the summer according to his vision of how he wanted us to play. With Andy Reid not consistently doing the business, we'd signed Wayne Routledge, a young lad from Crystal Palace, to play wide out right, though he could also switch to the other flank. But on his debut, a 2-0 away win at Portsmouth, a game I missed, he broke his foot.

By the time Routledge was fit to play again, his place wide out right had been secured by his understudy, and he was never able to break into the side after that, going out successfully on loan to Portsmouth and Fulham before being transferred to Aston Villa. The player who took Wayne's intended place wide right was a kid Tottenham had picked up in the fire sale at Leeds United when financial crisis forced them to sell some real talent. Aged just eighteen and only five foot five, Aaron Lennon was the little to his fellow Yorkshireman Michael Dawson's large.

Being small and young but covering a lot of ground, Aaron seldom had the puff to complete every game he started, but he had the pace and trickiness to get behind the opposing full-back to the byline, and was just what Martin wanted. That's when his management took off. Boom. He recognized he'd got someone young and hungry here who, if you get the ball out wide to him in a one-on-one situation, with his pace and enthusiasm and toughness despite his age, he was difficult to stop; he can get past his man and put the ball into an area. In training we used to work on getting the ball out to the wingers and crossing, and that's what Aaron loved doing. Martin used to say, 'Get the ball out wide – it's half a goal!' That was his saying because he was that confident that Lennon wide out right would beat his man and get the ball into the box.

On the left side of midfield we had a very different style of player new in at the club. With a young team, many of them new to the club, Martin Jol recognized that we could still do with some experience, and they don't come much more experienced than Edgar Davids – not just a legend but a lion. One of those great Surinam-born Dutch players, Edgar had been an engine and an inspiration for Ajax – where his manager, Louis van Gaal, had nicknamed him 'the Pitbull' – then Juventus, Barcelona and Inter Milan. When he arrived at Tottenham on a free transfer he was aged thirty-two but still hungry to win.

We were very excited to hear that he was coming to Tottenham. Sitting down in the canteen even before we'd kicked a ball, before he'd even trained with us, Edgar asked me, 'Can we win anything?' and I said, 'Yeah, we can, you know. I believe we can.' So he said, 'Good. That's what I want to hear.' From day one, he wasn't here for a jolly-up, he was there to win. That was his character – giving 100 per cent to be a winner.

In the gym he used to have a routine where he used to lift quite heavy weights the day before a game. This was new to us. None of us touched weights the day before a game; it was something that we'd done earlier in the week. And in the dressing room before games he'd get a ball and kick it into the wall, getting tighter and tighter until it was too wedged in to bounce, as if he was tackling the wall, getting the tension the way he wanted it in the leg.

Edgar gave us that bit of steel we needed on the left and in the middle of the park. His reputation scared opponents. When you're in the tunnel with Edgar with his dreadlocks and orange shades and his mean face on, you could sense the other team were having a little look at him in the line, and he would snarl! You felt good with him in your team and not theirs!

Edgar was very tough and tenacious but he loved ball skills too. You'd see him in adverts doing street football, stuff like that. Edgar worked closely with Ricardo Moniz, our skills coach, who Martin had brought in. Ricardo used to be a player and did a lot of good work with the club developing some of the younger players coming through into the first team, the reserve players. You saw that they all improved technically from working with him, especially the really young players at Tottenham, the kids of ten, eleven and twelve. Ricardo would be there for hours in the dome of the Spurs Lodge training ground, coaching them and teaching them tricks and skills.

Aside from Edgar giving us the scare factor that we needed at that time, Martin Jol also brought in the experience of left-back Lee Young-Pyo, who had played in World Cups for Korea, and, at right-back, Paul Stalteri had come from the German League, so you knew he had to have a certain mental toughness as well as defensive qualities.

Widely experienced players like that really benefited the young English talent we were nurturing at the club, including twenty-two-year-old Jermaine Jenas (JJ to everyone) who came in from Newcastle on the last day of the 2005 summer transfer window. Anthony Gardner was still around then, and JJ, Lennon, Carrick, Defoe, Dawson and I were all young but maturing, with quite a few of us in the England squad together. Lennon and, the following season, Tom Huddlestone were a little bit younger, so they were under the wings of the more established players like me, learning about the club and the history. Everyone got on well, and there was no hierarchy with the manager, and no egos, even though at first people were not sure what Edgar was going to be like, based on what you read, but he was good to have around the place. We were all on the same page, all moving in the right direction. We recognized we had a good little team brewing, a good balance of young, exciting players and experience. We felt we could finish in the top four.

Whereas under Glenn Hoddle we had a lot of players who were coming to the later stages of their career and a few young players who were just coming into the start of their careers, now under Martin we not only had a more even spread of experience, maturity and youth, but we also had players with similar interests, and that helped the team spirit. As well as lads from London like Defoe and me, Keane and Carrick had lived in London for a while, and Dawson and JJ were keen to join in as we enjoyed being young together in the capital city: the music, the games, the fun.

Playing cards on the coach and golf in the afternoon had faded away with the last players of Teddy Sheringham's generation. With more players from lots of different countries, backgrounds and cultures, now was the time of iPods, DVD players, computer games and personal gadgets. Our team coach was set up with an oval seating area at the back which could seat seven or eight people. The table was in the middle so you'd get a group discussion, players listening to music on headphones, players watching a movie.

It was a harmonious team and increasingly a winning team. With a month to go before the end of the season, we were lying fourth, with a serious shot for the first time of qualifying for the Champions League.

Playing Everton at Goodison Park was always tough under David Moyes, and after Robbie Keane put us ahead on the half-hour, we were hanging on for the next hour to secure all three points. On sixty-six minutes, Everton sent on big Duncan Ferguson from the bench to try to retrieve the game. Past his best by then, he was still a player who had a reputation as a very, very tough challenge for a defender; he loved a battle. I was never the most physical of defenders, but when he came on it didn't bother me. Maybe a few years earlier it might have been a different story, but now I felt in my prime. I felt I could move and run and jump and do it all, although he was really strong in the air. I beat him in the air a few times because he was a little bit older now and didn't have the same legs on him. Then, with Everton about to play the ball in for Ferguson, he and I were jostling early for it, and he just threw his arm back at me and said, 'Don't fucking touch me else I'll lay one on ya.' That was the first time I'd heard that kind of talk on the pitch; that was old school to me. The next header we went up for he beat me in the air because I was waiting for an elbow to come to my face. Just by his words and reputation, he put me off the next challenge, because I thought there was an elbow coming.

But we played well and ground it out at 1-0, and literally a minute or two before the final whistle I jumped up in our own box and felt a crack. It was a familiar feeling. I knew exactly what it was – the fourth metatarsal bone in the left foot. I came off the pitch straight away, knowing I would miss the rest of the season, and bitterly disappointed that I would not be part of the team as we fought to hang on to our top-four place in the League.

That broken metatarsal also kept me out of consideration for the England squad competing in that summer's World Cup finals in Germany. When, in a rerun of Euro 2004, which I had to miss, we went out on penalties to Portugal in the quarter-final, I felt I couldn't dwell too long on what might have been. Yet again, it was just one of those things.

Meanwhile, on the last day of the League season, if Tottenham beat West Ham at Upton Park, it wouldn't matter how many Arsenal scored at home against Wigan for the navy-blue half of North London to qualify for the Champions League in fourth ahead of the red half of North London in fifth. West Ham was a local derby but a winnable game, a game where we expected to go to and get the result that we needed.

Apart from me, JJ and Paul Stalteri were also out, so we arranged to meet up at the training ground and get driven down to Upton Park. We were a little bit anxious before the game because so much was riding on it, and there was nothing we could do to help. In the car we heard something on the news, that Tottenham players were ill. We texted a few players to see what was happening and found out that quite a few of the players felt like they had food poisoning.

It wasn't until we actually got down to the stadium and made our way to the visitors' changing room that we actually realized how much they were affected. The feeling walking into the changing room was almost as if it was after the game and we'd lost. The players were so ill that they had nothing in them. Their heads were down, nothing like what you'd expect before a huge game kicking off in the next hour. I was worried. I could see the players were really struggling with the sickness.

I had so much respect for them when they went out there and played through their sickness. We all know what it's like to have food poisoning – it's a nightmare scenario, and then to have to run around and try and play . . . You could see that they wanted to give everything, but they had nothing to give. The lads tried, but they just didn't have the fight in them. That we scored at all – from Jermain Defoe – was a miracle.

Watching your teammates go out there and try and give everything for the team but with nothing to give was sad. It was a quiet changing room after the game. Everyone was sad, and you knew what the players were thinking: we tried and we couldn't give any more.

We weren't exactly sure, but at the time it was put down to food poisoning affecting seven or eight players. It seemed that they'd all eaten the same meal at the hotel the night before – lasagne. Wild rumours circulated that an Arsenal or West Ham fan in the hotel kitchens had interfered with the food served to the Tottenham team. The press called it 'Lasagne-gate'. But when doctors ran tests, they found out that it was a virus that had spread like wildfire. That tiny little bug cost us dear.

Afterwards, the club went to great lengths to make sure that a group of players on a team didn't get affected by such an outbreak again. If a player showed signs of being ill, he would straight away be isolated from the rest of the group. We erred on the side of caution after 'Lasagne-gate'.

That final day of the season it just wasn't to be. It had ended in an anticlimax we couldn't have foreseen or prevented – but otherwise the season was Tottenham's best in years. After we got over the initial disappointment, the feeling was that we'd made big strides and were nearly there.

Tottenham had arrived as genuine contenders for the first time in I don't know how long. We knew we could push on.

RUNNING TO STAND STILL

Knocking on the door of big-time success brings its own pit-falls. While I was still an apprentice at Tottenham, Manchester United identified our best football brain, Teddy Sheringham, as a player who could help them push even higher. They were right: in 1999 Teddy made a huge difference to help them win the treble, which included the Champions League. Man U's gain was Tottenham's loss, and now they were back, yet again targeting our best football brain: Michael Carrick. And in the end, what they were offering was too much to refuse.

Just as Martin was trying to build a side that could compete with Man United at the top, he'd lost one of his best foundation stones. But in the intake of new players that summer of 2006 was one who, though a striker rather than a midfielder, had just as advanced a football brain: purchased from Bayer Leverkusen for £10 million, Dimitar Berbatov.

To be honest, at first I didn't know he was going to become as good as he did for the club. He was very laid-back in training. He played the game at his own tempo. He had a different style of play to anything I was used to. He was like a player beyond his years. He was never rushed, he was always composed. He liked to link up play, get out wide, get into the box in his own time. That's very different to the usual story in the Premier League, where everything's hustle and bustle. He calmed everything down when he played. You could see he had quality, but I wasn't sure how many goals he would score. I wasn't sure if he was quick enough or sharp enough to score as many goals as he did. I could see his quality, but we all saw as well that we'd probably have to adapt a bit to his style. After a slow start, it all began to click.

As lanky and languid as he was, the Bulgarian's touch was immaculate, his vision was acute, and he would ghost into space, from where he'd slot it away with cold-blooded precision. He soon began to build up an understanding with Robbie Keane, whose bustle balanced Berbatov's graceful economy of effort, and by the end of the season there wouldn't be too many to deny they were the best strike partnership in the country.

Also that summer, in came the young midfielder who Martin Jol saw as the man who would set into motion the attacks from out wide that he believed in so passionately: bought from Derby County, Tom Huddlestone. Martin really liked his passing ability. He had a special talent, was two-footed, very balanced and had the knack of playing the thirty-five-yard diagonal pass out to the wing. He could change the whole shape of the game with a pass, giving the winger time to get down the flank before playing a pinpoint ball to him. With his youth and inexperience at the top level, he didn't get his chance early in the season but he was bubbling in the background; you knew he would come through and get his chance.

We had lads from different places but we all got on really well, and that's what you want from your club. We were happy with the squad that we had, a good bunch to work with, and no bad eggs, no problems. We had good lads and a good spirit.

Yet again, though, I missed the start of the season. My right knee had been playing up and after cartilage surgery that summer I needed time to recover and get back to fitness. Then I got a run which included a great 2-1 home win against Chelsea, when I'm happy to say I managed to catch Arjen Robben, who had a good head start over me, as he raced to our goal, tackling him cleanly in our area. So at that point, November, I was pretty fit. But at Christmas my metatarsal started playing up, and I didn't play again until April.

As I've mentioned before, my frame, my structure, had a built in weakness. I've always had bow legs and flat feet, and that combination put a lot of pressure on the outside of my feet. I had foot orthotics made to put into my boots, but I really hated them. I like my boots to be pure. With these moulded insoles, they just felt different. You're used to standing in a certain way, feeling your feet that way, and all of a sudden the foot orthotics were correcting what you were used to. Which of course is what they're supposed to do. But I was stubborn. I tried them in training and in games, and they felt wrong. I just didn't feel right in them when I was playing. I felt they were going to put me off my game. I didn't feel like I could move around and play the way I wanted to. There was an ongoing battle to try to make me wear them. I would train and play without them but then felt the metatarsal playing up. I thought, this can't keep happening, so in the end I had to try to wear them and just play through them feeling wrong, which I did for a little while. Then I stopped again.

When the metatarsal was playing up, it was an ache beneath the bone, which felt as if it was on the verge of fracturing again. The ache in your foot wouldn't stop you from playing as such, but it stopped me because I felt it was a warning sign that the metatarsal would break if at all stressed. Our physio called this feeling a 'stress response'. So I'd tell the manager and medical staff that I'd better rest it for a while and not play for a week or two. I knew the feeling, and they trusted that I knew. I'd rest for a couple of weeks, thinking that would do the trick. But at the end of the fortnight it would still feel the same. I would go out with the fitness coach for a little run, a bit of ball work, to see how it felt. But every time I tried, it didn't feel like it was improving.

So should I even consider risking a return to full training to get match fit? Our thinking was that if I did that despite the ache not going away, and the metatarsal was to go, that would be a little bit silly. So we'd rest it another two weeks. And so on. Worse still, after a while I began to get an ache in my other foot too.

Nor had the problems with my right knee been solved for good by that summer's cartilage operation. I had daily exercises to keep it flexible, and it had to be monitored and managed closely by the club's medical staff. But that season, it was not the knee but the metatarsal stress response that kept me out for nearly four months from Boxing Day 2006 after we beat Aston Villa. In the end, I felt that enough was enough. It got to a stage where I felt I had to come back and play, and if it was going to go, it was going to have to go. I would take the risk.

When I came back that April of 2007, it was in the UEFA Cup quarter-final against the holders, Sevilla. They were a really good side then, with a good manager, Juande Ramos, and a good pedigree for winning cup competitions.

I travelled with the team to the first leg out in Seville and had my first training session with them for months, though I didn't play. It was a tough, intimidating stadium to go to, and police in helmets and riot gear were wading into the seats at the Spurs end, hitting fans left and right with their batons. We lost 2-1 but had a real go.

After the game we were on the bus, and some of our fans spotted us and were pointing, clapping and waving. The police were pushing them away, but one of the fans continued to clap, and all of a sudden one of the policemen banged him in the face with his baton, and kept on hitting him. We jumped off the bus, protesting it was out of order. The fan wasn't doing anything wrong and he'd stepped back from the bus as it was trying to leave the ground, so he wasn't obstructing anybody. All the police were in uniform, so looked identical, and I think the policeman who'd assaulted the fan sneaked off because he knew he'd done wrong. We took the fan into the changing room to see the doctor. He'd had his teeth smashed out of his mouth. It was horrific. He'd done nothing at all to deserve being beaten up and injured like that.

After an investigation, the Spanish club apologized for the thuggish behaviour of the local police.

A week later, on 12 April, we had Sevilla back for the second leg at White Hart Lane. It was my first game back, my first since Christmas. I was nowhere near ready but I felt I could help the team overturn the deficit and go through to the semis, and the manager wanted me to have a go too because we had a load of injuries in defence: Gardner, Stalteri and both left-back options, Lee Young-Pyo and Benoît Assou-Ekotto, were all out. But in the first twenty minutes I was off the pace in the game, and after eight minutes we were 2-0 down, their first coming from our midfielder Steed Malbranque, when he lashed at the ball in our area and it came off the outside of his boot, and their second goal from our former striker Freddie Kanouté.

Really, I had no right to be playing. I'd hardly had any training after being over three months out and I was off the pace, but gradually eased into the game and got better. We got the game back to two-all and were chasing for the third goal, but it didn't come. Sevilla went on to win the competition for the second season in a row.

It was a new experience for us, a good experience playing against a good side, and we took a bit of heart from the fact that we had come back from 2-0 down to level the score and then really put them on the back foot as we looked for our next goal.

Tottenham ended the 2006/2007 season fifth for the second time in a row. We had consolidated the huge progress we'd made in Martin Jol's first full season, and that without Michael Carrick, who had pulled all the strings in midfield. But we had racked up five fewer points than the season before, and had not given Arsenal much of a race; yet again they finished fourth, but eight points ahead of us.

What none of us players knew was that the club's board were worried that we were slipping rather than progressing. Like us, they'd been impressed by Sevilla, a club challenging Spanish football's dominance by Real Madrid and Barcelona. This was a real achievement, given their resources, and the board were particularly impressed by their manager, Juande Ramos. But we players knew none of this as we prepared for the 2007/2008 season.

NO ONE EXPECTS THE SPANISH INQUISITION . . .

In the early summer I was called up for England duty for the B team against Albania and, for the seniors, a friendly 1-1 against Brazil and a 3-0 win over Estonia in the European Championship qualifying stages.

Brazil was the first game at the new Wembley, and against such a prestigious team with the likes of Ronaldinho and Kaká everyone wanted to be involved. I was delighted to start the game. The pitch wasn't great, not as good as for the Carling Cup final seven months later.

Steve McClaren was England manager. Before him, Sven-Göran Eriksson had taken a back seat while Steve took all the training sessions, so that made the transition easy when he became manager, and he continued to take all the training sessions. The lads all respected him as a coach and as a manager, and we all got on well with him. He was easy to talk to, and I liked him.

All through that time the big question for the England manager was whether you could play both Lampard and Gerrard in the same side. I think both of them would have played better in a freer midfield with an extra centre midfield player; it would have made their jobs easier if there was someone holding behind them. Gerrard is an all-round midfield player, so I see him play the holding role, and it's something that he's doing more and more as he gets older. But he's still got that quality driving forward from midfield. Lampard likes to do that too, and at this stage getting into the box was his main strength. Again, now he's a bit older he's also dropped in a bit deeper, so they've become similar again. But they're both top players, and there's no reason why their partnership for England shouldn't have been able to work. That it didn't hampered Steve McClaren's England.

As I say, the lads all liked and respected him, and in theory we should have done a lot better than we did for him. It was disappointing the way he left the England set-up, facing a lot of harsh criticism from the media mocking him for standing under the golf umbrella when England were beaten by Croatia at a rainy Wembley and so failed to qualify for the 2008 Euros. I felt very sorry for him.

Earlier in the qualifying rounds, when we beat Estonia 3-0, I aggravated my right knee cartilage problem, and the decision was taken to look into more radical surgery to treat it.

Microfracture surgery was recommended as offering me the best chance to overcome my worsening chronic knee problem. Normally cartilage doesn't regrow when it's torn, and since the cartilage is the lubricant tissue that allows the knee joint to operate flexibly, torn and worn cartilage means pain, swelling and stiffness under even ordinary stress, never mind the stresses of running around for over ninety minutes of football, or even of a normal training session.

Microfracture surgery wasn't something that I knew about, but I had a little look at it. Rather than drilling into the knee, which is what the procedure used to entail, my microfracture surgery involved repeatedly hammering the hyaline cartilage in the knee with a very small tool to fracture it on a minute scale, and stimulate the regrowth of fresh cartilage. Though the new cartilage is not as strong and hard-wearing as that which had been lost, it's much better than nothing. Pioneered in the US less than twenty-five years ago and refined as a technique in the years since, microfracture surgery has offered a lifeline to sportsmen, most commonly basketball players, whose knees have suffered from the stresses of their sport. But there weren't too many footballers I could find who'd had the operation, Being a hoops fan, though, I'd seen a few basketball players who'd had it. I knew that some had never really come back properly from microfracture surgery. But I needed something done to the knee and I was determined to find my way through whatever risks I was taking. Doing nothing was not an option.

The operation itself, under general anaesthetic, does not take long, but afterwards the healing process, rehabilitation and physiotherapy takes many weeks. You have to be very self-disciplined to do exactly what you're told for it to have the best chance of working.

Mr – now Professor – Fares Haddad, who'd operated on me previously and seen my knee over the years, performed the procedure at the Princess Grace Hospital on 19 June 2007. I trusted him to go in and do whatever needed doing. Straight away, hours after the surgery, you're trying to keep it loose. Literally when I came round from the operation I was on a machine to promote full extension in my leg. It's key not to let your leg lock without it being fully extended because that shortens your stride so you can't run properly. My challenge was to regain full knee extension and rebuild the muscle mass of the quadriceps and hamstrings without overloading the knee. This is a tough task over a prolonged period, especially with ninety-minute games making it difficult to perform any activity for two to three days afterwards, when ideally I would be doing exercises every day.

After the microfracture surgery, my knee was never the same; it was a different knee. It's a very strange sensation, hard to describe. It's not only very stiff but it feels like you have two entirely different knees: one you're fully aware of and in control of, the other one you're not. It's almost like it's not your knee, but a robot's knee.

It takes a while to come back from the actual surgery. Some players take longer than others. Everyone at the club knew that, even with rehab going well, I would yet again miss the start of the new season. Rehab was not about getting back to my old self but learning how to deal with a new self, one where the right knee didn't feel right.

But I was always one of those people who would play if he could. By then I couldn't remember the last time I'd felt 100 per cent, really great in a game. So I was aware that the knee was not ideal, and I was already thinking about getting it right at a later stage. But for now, I had to try to overcome this sense of not being right and get on with getting fit enough to play.

As if this problem wasn't bad enough, the manager made no secret of his view that the team did not defend as well when I was out injured. He would never try to pressure me into coming back too soon, but when he praised me – making me feel that when I played, we'd be fine – that made me feel guilty when I couldn't play.

And at the start of the 2007/2008 season, while I was still recovering from the surgery and so watching games from behind the bench rather than playing them, we were conceding more than we were scoring, and the results were poor. Apart from beating a relegation-bound Derby County 4-0 in August, Tottenham didn't win a League game until November. By then Martin Jol was gone.

Whenever a manager is sacked it's strange. But this one was really strange. Having come fifth again the previous season, we'd also qualified again for the UEFA Cup. At our group stage home game against the Spanish side Getafe, managed by

Michael Laudrup, on Thursday, 25 October, I was sitting in my normal spot behind the bench when I didn't play. About twenty minutes in I got this text on my phone from a friend watching the game on TV who'd seen a newsflash: 'Your manager's been sacked.' I'm thinking this is crazy, so I obviously told a few people around me at the time. And then you started to sense a strange atmosphere in the crowd; you sensed something was in the air, that they'd heard something too, that something had happened while we were playing the game. The atmosphere just went so quiet, so dead.

We went in at half-time and put the TV on in the manager's room next to the players' dressing room, where normally at half-time he'd circle around waiting for everyone to be sat down ready and then he would come in and talk to you. The TV was on, showing the game, but I didn't really get a proper chance to see it. We went into the team talk, as was normal to do, and then went back out to our seats behind the bench for the second half. The crowd was singing Martin's name, cheering for him and trying to get behind him. But despite all the team's efforts on the Getafe goal, it was the Spanish team, then in the bottom three of La Liga, who nicked it 2-1. We were still in the competition, but it was a miserable evening.

After the game we sat in the changing room, waiting for the manager to come trotting in a few minutes later, as was the routine. But he was taking his time, and everyone was starting to get a bit suspicious. Everyone was looking at each other –

what's happening, what's going on? We were waiting and waiting for Martin to come in the room.

The wait was going on and on, and then I think it was Damien Comolli, who'd replaced Frank Arnesen as the club's director of football when the Dane went to Chelsea, who came into the room. He said that Martin would be leaving. We were all shocked and disappointed. Then our skills coach Ricardo Moniz stood up and said, 'We can't accept this.' He was very cut up about it. I said to him, 'What can we do? You know there's nothing we can do.' It was a very weird situation.

Five minutes later Martin came in and shook everyone's hands and wished us good luck.

Clearly it had been a decision taken in the boardroom upstairs. The chairman and board were very ambitious and wanted to see consistent progress, and quickly. Yes, the results so far that season had been poor, but you couldn't really put your finger on why. The manager always said we were a much better team, much harder to beat, when I was playing, and of course I wasn't playing. Even so, we still had good players, so there was no reason for us to be poor. I know that some fans and journalists said we didn't look in shape or very fit going into the new season. That's not how the team looked to me from my position watching from behind the bench. Maybe when you're on the outside looking in it seems different.

Yes, we came into the season a bit flat, but not for want of a good period of pre-season preparation. We'd had a good pre-season, winning all seven games. But we hadn't overdone it: we'd played eight pre-season games the previous summer and got off to a much better League start.

By then, though, I was no longer doing proper pre-seasons with the team. I had five or six years where I had no real pre-season, just doing my own work. It's not ideal but different players can adapt to different situations. Not only are training and pre-season preparations tailored to players in different positions, but individual players need particular approaches to attain their different kinds of fitness. Not everyone can run round for half an hour, for example. As a defender you're never really running constantly; you're running in bursts. As I got older I learned to work in bursts because that's how it works in games. Some players need a good pre-season under their belts otherwise they don't really get their season up and running. By then I understood my body, and if I said that I didn't think that I should do this run, the coaches knew that I could break down if I tried. As you get older, you get to learn about your body

The main thing as a player is how you feel. You can moan about training work, running too much, doing too much, but if you go into the game and you're feeling good then you know it's all worth it. It all depends on the end product. As you get older you learn about what you don't like and what you do like and what actually works for you when it comes to actually playing the game. With my injury problems making my situation within the team really unusual, I'd learned to manage myself.

But not everyone agreed. The new manager, for example.

When Juande Ramos came in from Sevilla he tried to change everything. It was a shock to us all. Replacing a manager as popular with the players and fans as Martin Jol, perhaps he felt he had to come in and make a bold statement and shake things up. I don't think he got off on the right foot with the team by coming in and changing so much so quickly. The first few months under his management were difficult.

The first thing Ramos said to us was that we were all overweight. He didn't tell us in the nicest way either. We had players from all over the world but he made us feel as if we were fat English yobs eating chips and drinking beer all day. I don't know if that's what he thought of us. It was a strange one. It was disrespectful.

The players weren't happy. I think there was only one who didn't have to lose weight, and that was Jermaine Jenas. He had to put some weight on. So, no fried foods in the canteen, no ketchup or sauce, and no juice, just water. And they monitored our weight. We had to lose some kilos and stay below a certain weight otherwise we faced fines. Our goalkeeper, Paul Robinson, slimmed down loads.

Ramos saw our weight as really important. When he first came in he said that, combined, we were something like 100 kilos heavier than Sevilla combined. We tried to explain to him that there were good reasons for that. This is England, we said, with a different style of football; you're not playing in the sun, and you need a bit of meat on your bones. And we added that there was nothing to say the Tottenham players were not bigger and stronger built than some of the Sevilla guys.

All the weight stuff made no sense to me. Yes, you always get one or two players a manager might take a look at and say that they need to shed a few kilos. But to say a whole team needed to lose weight seemed to me more a case of coming in and trying to find problems rather than really solving anything.

In charge of implementing Ramos's weight policy was his sidekick, Marcos Alvarez. He was a fitness coach for Sevilla but when he came to us he had a big role across a lot of areas, and I'm not sure that that was his real strength. I don't think he really knew football that well. For me he was just a fitness coach.

Before Ramos and Alvarez, Sam Erith, who eventually went on to Man City as their fitness coach, had measured our weights and found that seven to eight per cent of mine was body fat, which, he said, was as close to the correct ratio as you can get. So I didn't have a problem with my weight, and I think a lot of other people felt the same way about theirs. But when, under Alvarez, I stepped on the scales, according to his formula of what my weight should be in proportion to my height, I was marked as almost obese. I don't know how Alvarez was doing it, but I obviously wasn't fat. If you judge a sportsman to be overweight based on a ratio of their weight and height, the result can be misleading. Everyone's bodies are different, with different muscles and bone density.

Maybe some players were happy with this crash diet policy but the majority weren't. Players were often hungry and would often smuggle food into our hotel rooms before games, especially sweet things. So it was a difficult initial period, and the training was hard too, harder than we'd ever had.

Ramos's key to success was about coming in and changing the diet and the fitness straight away, but to make such dramatic changes during the season will affect the players' legs in games. It's not ideal to go through a period of struggling in games, and only a little while down the line hopefully seeing the benefits. That's why such big changes are normally undertaken in pre-season.

When Ramos came in I was recovering from my microfracture surgery but could play as long as I had two or three days for the knee to recover afterwards. I certainly couldn't train normally every day and still be able to play. So I had to try and explain to him that I didn't train. His reaction was that no one doesn't train and still plays. It wasn't going to happen. In my first training session under Ramos I had to go beyond what I wanted to do. I tried to explain to him that I could actually do some training but it would be detrimental to my knee, and if he wanted me to train, he needed to ask himself whether he wanted me at the weekend. I told him that if he didn't want me at the weekend, I could have had two or even three training sessions during that week.

For a manager, it's not a situation you come across every day and, new at the club, he didn't really seem to understand. Nor did Marcos Alvarez. The whole idea was alien to them; it was not the norm. The physio tried to explain the situation to them, but Ramos wasn't really having it.

I ended up forcing myself to train. One of the first training sessions was some kind of fitness thing, and I knew it was not really what I needed and I shouldn't be out there slogging around. I did it, but my knee blew up. After that, they understood that I needed to manage my own fitness. Before a game, I occasionally took the painkilling anti-inflammatory Celebrex, though not as religiously as I ended up taking it towards the end.

In games and in limited training, I'm having to prove myself to him because he doesn't know me, doesn't know if I'm any good or not. I've got to get on the training pitch to try and show him what I can do. But what I didn't need was to do the hard running, the long slogs. As a defender you run in bursts, and that's how I needed to limit my running in training sessions to preserve the knee for the game itself.

Finally there came a point when Ramos trusted that I could play but not train. So then he started to pick the games he wanted me to play. And there weren't too many that 2007/2008 season. But two stand out as among the greatest of my entire career.

For all the disruption and unhappiness, it was under Ramos that season that, as team captain, I took part in my one winning Wembley final and lifted the one major trophy in all my years at the club. My knee was crocked, I could hardly play or train, and I was getting more and more detached from the team spirit which had been such a buzz and support for me. Yet this was also the season that finally gave me the feeling of triumph and glory that every footballer craves.

GLORY AT LAST!

My record for the whole of the 2007/2008 season is played ten, won five, drew three, lost two. As I mentioned, our new manager, Juande Ramos, started to pick my games for me, and he was very picky. Only four of those games were in the League, and one of them was an amazing 6-4 win over Reading. We were 2-1 down on the hour when Ramos took me off for Jermain Defoe, and the floodgates opened up at both ends, Berbatov netting four by the final whistle. I also played in another high-scoring game, 4-4 against Chelsea at White Hart Lane. Again, when we were chasing the game, I was substituted in exchange for a striker, this time our big-money signing Darren Bent. In both games, I'm happy to say, the manager's decision to sacrifice me for a goalscorer paid off. But the two games that season which will forever live in my memory and, I'm sure, in the memories of all Tottenham fans watching live or on TV that season, were fought against our two fiercest London rivals in the League Cup.

We'd beaten Middlesbrough, Blackpool and Manchester City to make it to the semi-final, where we were drawn against

Arsenal, with the first leg at the Emirates Stadium on 9 January 2008. On five minutes I got the ball, played it and continued the run. But just when I almost got played in, my legs turned to jelly. I'd run sixty metres and there were eighty-five minutes left! So, despite my confidence going into attack, my lack of full match-fitness meant I had to learn to conserve my energy for the defending. But we were definitely the better side, with JJ scoring in the first half and the home team lucky to get an equalizer quite late on.

Ramos had seen enough of Arsenal in that game to know what to do to beat them, and we practised throughout the next week how we were going to play. After that first game, he said that when we won the ball back we just had to run into the space behind them, and that was the way to kill them. Ramos set us up the way he had set up his great Cup-winning Sevilla team, and I think this is why he wanted me to play in the semi – he knew I could quickly pick out a pass from defence to our fast attacking players. We had the pace, and I think Ramos saw Lennon as a little right-winger in the mould of the Sevilla player Jesús Navas, now at Man City, who is really small and quick. We were going to spring on them when they were on the ball, we were going to flood them, really break on them. And every time we won the ball back, he wanted our players to fly forwards at pace. That's what we worked on extra-hard before the return leg. And in the game that's exactly what we did.

Sometimes you have those games when it's just magical. I had one earlier in my career when we played Chelsea at White Hart Lane, and that evening was another where you come out of the blocks, and the other team just can't live with you, and you run rampant. Our tails were up from the first minute to the last, and to reach a final, and to reach it on our home ground in front of our own fans against one of our biggest rivals by such a big score – 5-1 – was one of my best days ever in a Spurs shirt.

For all the upset his attitude to diet and fitness generated among the players, none of us would deny that tactically Ramos was good, especially over two legs. He would learn things from the first game and work out how to win the second. We trusted him to set up the right tactics to go and get results in the second leg.

Ramos was an excellent cup manager. He'd won the UEFA Cup with Sevilla and really focused on that with Tottenham too, as well as the League Cup. Given that when he arrived, a third of the League season had been played and he'd had little time to study in detail our League opponents to work out the best tactics for each game, he probably calculated that the cups were always more likely to bring him instant success at his new club rather than trying to catch up in a league he didn't really know.

As a strategy for the 2007/2008 season it certainly paid off. In both Arsenal games I partnered Michael Dawson in central defence. But in the final I was to play alongside the club's new January transfer window signing from Middlesbrough, Jonathan Woodgate.

I'd played with Alan Smith in the young England sides, and he talked about Woodgate as a top player even then, which I found out for myself when I played with Woody once or twice for the England Under-18s. As a player he was pretty similar to me, so we would hopefully be vying to get into the England squad and maybe playing together some day.

Making his reputation at Leeds and Newcastle, at Real Madrid Woody had struggled with injuries, but he came back to Middlesbrough and showed really good form, with a particularly good game at White Hart Lane. Obviously Ramos would have known about his quality and experience from Madrid, and that's probably why he went after him.

And yes, as a young player at Leeds, Woody got into some trouble, and what was reported wasn't pretty. But I wasn't worried, and the subject never came up. Every player has made mistakes, and I can personally vouch that Woody's a good guy, a good character, good to have around the place. He's full of banter, and the lads loved him.

I think initially Ramos was brought in to change the team and the mentality of the players. He tried to put his stamp on the team and make a difference as soon as he came in. But in the months after we began to see a nice guy who liked the team spirit. Two days before the League Cup final, sponsored by Carling, was played on 24 February 2008, he got the team together for an extended bonding session. It was just the squad of around twenty-three of us, no wives, girlfriends or family. Normally you only meet up the evening before a very big game like a Wembley final, so this long weekend together wasn't something that we'd done before. We weren't quite sure what to expect. We trained on the Friday, then went to the hotel.

We stayed at the Grove in Watford, a lovely hotel where many of us had stayed before, so we were comfortable there. There's a friendly, relaxed atmosphere, our rooms were all along the same corridors, and we had our own space, so it was perfect for us.

Around the hotel was a big grassy area and a lot of fields, so we had plenty of space to relax. The manager wanted to let us take our minds off the game, take the stress away and let us relax. So after light training on the Saturday, he organized an activity fun day, with a go-kart track set up just for us. Just as he'd planned, we really had a good laugh and bonded. The Saturday night before the game as well we had a little casino set up. We weren't gambling with real money – it was just a bit of a laugh for the lads.

Being relaxed and together helped us to bond, but at the same time the game was never going to leave our minds. But we had a laugh and it was an enjoyable stay. I think it really set us up to go into the game feeling good about it.

On the morning of the game itself I had a bit of a shock to

the system. Reading the sports pages of the Sunday papers, I was taken aback to see speculation that, because I'd been struggling with the knee, the League Cup final might be the last game of my career.

This was the first time I'd seen my name linked to any thought of quitting. I'd never for one second thought about retiring. So now I had that extra motivation going into the game. I wanted to show people that I was far from finished. I hadn't played since the semi-final, and my mind was on making the final. I'd worked hard to make sure that I was going to be there. I was fit to play and now I went into the game determined to prove to people that I still had some years in me yet.

At the two-day bonding, relaxation and preparation stay at the Grove Hotel, we didn't know who was going to play in the final itself. The manager was keeping his options open with the full squad of players.

As far as his tactics against Chelsea were concerned, we were well aware of their threat. We weren't sure who they were going to play, but whoever it was, they had attacking options: Drogba, Kalou, Anelka, Wright-Phillips and Joe Cole. And you knew Lampard scored goals from midfield, a big part of their game. Any time you play Chelsea, when Lampard's at his best, he's a big goal threat for them arriving in the box. If you can eliminate him, they've got other players who can score goals. As defenders, Woody and I were confident we could do a job on

Drogba. But we needed our midfield players to stop Lampard from surprising us, popping up in the box.

Going into the game, we'd done our preparation, obviously looking at their threats. But also we looked at what could we do to hurt them. With Ramos, our game plan was based on pace. When we were attacking teams, he really wanted us to go with the pace and the energy we had. In central midfield Didier Zokora and Jermaine Jenas were good athletes, able to go up and down the pitch and get around Lampard, and they did a great job on the day. And playing wide, we had Aaron Lennon and Steed Malbranque, players with good legs, good energy. We felt we could hurt them with pace; that was the key for us. Chelsea were a team that liked to play at their own tempo and didn't like pace. If we could counter them with pace, we had a really good chance in the game.

We reckoned we had another edge too. Going into the game, we were aware of the fact that Avram Grant probably wasn't the most popular choice as manager among the Chelsea fans and maybe players too. Obviously Chelsea always had this ongoing issue with managers and the dressing room – it had been going on forever – while we all felt we had a really good team spirit and hoped that we could use that to cause an upset.

We'd also beaten them the season before in the League. For years we couldn't beat them, so now we had the belief that, if we did the right things, we could beat them again. That was a big factor in helping us win this final too.

But of course it would be tight.

Coming out onto the pitch at Wembley to warm up, we realized we had another edge: the Tottenham fans. Even the atmosphere on the day was to our advantage because our fans were just singing and cheering and roaring us on at a different level to the Chelsea fans. The fans drove us on, they were there for us, they were behind the team, and when the game kicked off the team was playing well. We could really feel a sense of togetherness among the players and the fans, and that helped us on the day, no doubt about it.

But then, slightly against the run of play, we went behind.

You're always aware when there's a player in the opposing team who can score free kicks. You go into the game thinking: we don't want to give them too many opportunities from outside the box. Everybody knew about Drogba's free kicks. With his power and accuracy, Drogba had a technique for free kicks that could cause problems, so you try to limit the opportunities you give him. Zokora had already given away a free kick before, and Drogba's free kick got close. So it was disappointing when Zokora made the tackle again and gave away another free kick. That's where you want your players to be intelligent, stand on their feet at the right time.

The second time Drogba stepped up he made no mistake. It was a great goal, and it hurt. I remember the reaction of some of the players. We felt down for that split second. We'd actually played well in the first half, and then to concede from a dead-ball situation where you're a little bit helpless, at that moment it did hurt.

Going in 1-0 down against Chelsea when you've played well in the first half could have created the fear that we'd given our best – and we probably felt that we had, that we'd had our best chances against them – and still they'd punished us. But what I was proud of was the fact that at half-time there was still a belief that we could win it.

That belief showed when we came back out in the second half. We continued doing exactly what we had been doing before, and we eventually got our reward with the penalty. I'm not sure, even to this day, that it was any more than a 50-50 penalty. But we were putting pressure on, getting in good areas and we felt as players that something was coming. We were going to get our reward, and we did. Obviously Berbatov, the coolest man in the stadium, slotted it away and made it look easy. From the moment the ball went into the back of the net, we went up another level of belief. Sometimes when you've been playing well you just need that goal to let you know that, if you keep knocking, that ball can and will go into the net. Once that ball went in we knew for sure that this was a game we could win.

So it went to extra time. It wasn't ideal for me to be going into 120 minutes after not playing for a good while, so for the whole of extra time I was cramping up. As usual, I'd taken some anti-inflammatories before the game, so as far as I was concerned there was no chance of me coming off the pitch. I was out there and I still felt I had enough in me to battle through.

We went ahead four minutes into extra time. We were awarded a free kick from wide left outside their area, and with our height Woody and I went up for it. JJ delivered up a great ball, Woody jumped up, and Chelsea's keeper Cech parried it into his face to bounce back into the goal.

We didn't care how the hell the ball went in, it was there! It was just a great feeling. Now we had something to hang onto, and that's where the team spirit came into it. We'd worked so hard to get to extra time and now we'd finally got our lead. We couldn't let this one slip.

Naturally the game turned after the goal because they were chasing, throwing caution to the wind, and we were just hanging on in there at times. Paul Robinson made a great save from Joe Cole, and there were a few scrambles in the box. Our difficulty was in hanging onto that lead for the last twenty-six minutes. You can't just keep giving the ball back to Chelsea every time you repel an attack because you're going to have to deal with the situation again and again. We had to get the ball wide, where we had the likes of Jenas, who could run the length of the pitch once he opened his legs, or to Lennon, who can get the ball down the pitch and bring the team up with him, or to Berbatov, with the way he could hold up a ball. He really put in an effort for the team; I saw him in a few places on the pitch I'd never seen him before, even full-back positions. When you see players doing that, it rubs off on everyone else.

Towards the end of the game Jenas got the ball down towards the right-hand side, and that's what you wanted to see – the ball deep in their half. Once the ball was in their half you can try to get up the field.

Because I was struggling with cramp – and me and Woody weren't the two fittest guys in the world – the manager decided to go three in the middle at the back. He took Robbie Keane off and sent on Younès Kaboul for extra height, speed and defensive power, since the ball was going to be coming into the box. As defenders you know that that's where your headers are vital; any time you don't win a header now, there's a 50-50 ball, and their players will be chasing round the back for the flick-ons. If you don't win a header in the box, with the number of bodies they've piled forward, there could be an opportunity to score. So that's where you needed the likes of Kaboul with his size to come on fresh, win an important header at an important time and stem the flow of the attacks.

It was backs to the wall, digging deep and trying to see it out to the whistle. Every time you clear the ball you're looking at the clock, and it seems to be at a standstill. Just as they were mounting another attack where they actually looked like they were going to score, hitting the post, the final whistle went.

As soon as that whistle went, we were off on our celebrations. You could see the feeling of togetherness within the group of players. It was a great, great moment. The first person I went to was Woody, obviously close to me on the pitch – we just hugged each other. And then on to the next person.

It was mayhem on the pitch as everyone surrounded the players. There were Chelsea players down on the ground, defeated and drained. Though I'd always said that if I were to win something I'd go and shake every opposition player's hand, your first reaction when it happens is to find a teammate first and celebrate. So the Tottenham players were grabbing each other and celebrating with each other. It was a lot of our players' first trophy, and I think that chance to win something for the first time accounted for the difference between the two teams' desire to win on the day. We didn't want to let that feeling go.

And I felt relief. I felt like I'd done it, I'd finally won something. I think that's how a lot of the players felt.

Once we'd celebrated, we went to the side of the pitch and got briefed on what to do. Chelsea went up first as runners-up, and then we went up. It seemed such a long way up to be presented with the cup and our winners' medals; it felt like it took forever to get up there. As we were walking up the stairs there were fans reaching out. You go missing round the back up the stairs and then you pop up again up the top. At this stage I was exhausted; I was just trying to get up those stairs to the trophy.

I went first, alongside Robbie. He'd been team captain for lots of games during the season, so that's why I wanted to lift it with him. He was a big character in the team, a big influence; we'd been at Tottenham a long time together and we felt l ike we'd been through a lot of upheavals, and now it was our moment. We felt we'd finally done it. It was so nice to share the triumph with Robbie and the rest of the team.

You lift the cup to show the fans, and the pandemonium level goes up another notch. Then you go back onto the pitch to run a lap of honour with the cup, and it's all a bit of a blur after that. You've got your medal on, you're still celebrating, still hugging your teammates, you have the team photo, there's champagne sprayed everywhere.

I felt such relief after reading the paper that morning and feeling so hurt that people thought I was actually finished. It had been a tough time for me with the knee. I knew the knee wasn't right. I was playing despite the knee not being how I wanted it to be. But I was determined to make this final, I was determined to play, and I was determined to show that I could still perform.

And I had.

ATTACKING THE MOUNTAIN

After we won the League Cup, the team dropped a lot of points in the Premier League. People reckoned it was a long hangover. I was not involved, since the manager was still picking my games, and they were all cup-ties. He'd won the UEFA Cup twice already with his previous side, Sevilla, and at Tottenham wanted a second item of silverware to put alongside the pot we won at Wembley. That would have been quite a first season for Juande Ramos had we pulled it off for him.

Sadly, on 12 March 2008, against the Dutch side PSV Eindhoven, we could only draw the two-legged tie, meaning penalties would decide who went through. On the hour, as we chased the goal that would bring the tie back on terms, the manager took me off and brought on Aaron Lennon to give us another attacking option, which paid off when Berbatov scored. So when it went to pens, I sat watching just as nervously as the Tottenham fans were as the shoot-out turned into a Mexican stand-off. With penalty shoot-outs being a bit of a Spurs hoodoo, we blinked first, losing 6-5.

Straight away, as the manager and I had agreed would be

the case as soon as we either won the UEFA Cup or were knocked out, I was off. I went on a world tour. But not for fun and relaxation. I was searching for something to make my knee better. I'd struggled all season, and though I had the joy of captaining the team as we won a Wembley final, the prospect of playing so few games the following season was not one I would accept without doing everything I could first to improve my condition.

My new Tottenham partner that spring wasn't Woody or Michael Dawson or any centre-back. It was club physio, Wayne Diesel. He's South African, and it was his country we flew to first; we flew to Johannesburg – for just one day. The specialists we saw there weren't the only ones who were talking about how I might need further operations. Given all the problems that had followed the microfracture procedure, more surgery was the option of last resort as far as I was concerned. Then we went to America, first to Phoenix, Arizona. I was there on the invitation and advice of the basketball star, Steve Nash. He plays for the LA Lakers now but in 2008 was in the form of his life for the Phoenix Suns. In successive years he was voted the National Basketball Association Most Valuable Player, a multiple winner like such legends as Magic Johnson and Michael Jordan. A Canadian national born in South Africa to an English dad, Steve is a massive Tottenham fan (even though the Suns' jinx team back then were the San Antonio Spurs!), and he actually came to Spurs Lodge back around 2006 and trained with the first team. Me being a big basketball fan, we hit it off.

Hearing of my knee problem, Steve had reached out to me and really looked after me while I was out there. I spent some time with the Suns' medical team because one of their players, Amar'e Stoudemire, had had the microfracture surgery, so their physio team had the kind of specialist experience that might help me.

Wanting to see as many different people as we could to get the widest range of advice, Wayne and I then flew out to LA to see Dr Bert Mandelbaum, the highly qualified and eminent orthopaedic surgeon, knee specialist and sports injury expert. He had a look at the knee, but he too, like most of the other medical experts, talked about further surgery.

It's not that I thought that the microfracture operation the previous summer had been a failure or had made my knee worse rather than better. The operation was needed back then; if I'd not had it I don't know how long I could have continued being able to play. But when you come round and the knee feels different, it's not ideal. So I was keen not to go down the surgery route again. I just wanted to have a good time rehabing it. You've got to trust your own instincts and that was the route I wanted to go down.

So after flying around the world to a few places, I didn't really come back with much.

By then it was the end of the season, and we were no closer

to a solution that was acceptable to me. But then Juande Ramos suggested someone he knew and rated highly. That it took so long for the recommendation to be made might tell you something about the general lack of communication and coordination during his time as manager. So off Wayne and I flew to Barcelona, to the long-established clinic for treating football injuries, the Mutualidad de Futbolistas Catalanes, to see their top man, Dr Ramón Cugat. He's worked not only with Barcelona players but footballers from all over Spain and Europe, Xavi, Puyol, Villa and Torres among them. Dr Cugat had a couple of ideas he thought could help, none of them surgical, so I decided to follow the path he recommended.

Dr Cugat wanted me to spend some time at the clinic, so I packed up my bags and spent a month out in Barcelona.

For that month I worked twice a day with Emili Ricart, a little Spanish guy who worked closely with Dr Cugat. They'd previously been at FC Barcelona, and Emili returned there as club physio a year or so after he treated me. He was someone who'd seen a lot of knees and knew football.

Flying back to Barcelona for the month's stay, rather than Wayne Diesel, it was Geoff Scott, another physio at Tottenham, who accompanied me. I remember going to the place where I was going to be staying, then going to see Emili and the area where I was going to be spending all my time, a mountainous little place outside Barcelona called Terrassa, and feeling that I wanted to go straight home! Geoff and I had a bit of a laugh about it. He was off to Vegas next, and I was left there on my own in the middle of nowhere! When I said goodbye to him, I wanted to cry, 'Please take me with you!'

But I had to get my knee right. That was the most important thing for me.

The first few days were tough. I was bored. It had to be a case of: while I'm here, let's just get my head down and do the work. With Emili, I was rehabing twice a day, the first session from ten in the morning until one. Then I'd have some lunch back at the hotel and a little sleep. Then at around four we were back at work for another three hours. By the time I'd got back in the evening and had something to eat, I was too tired to socialize. It was a case of chilling out and waiting for the next day to come around.

One of the first things Emili got me doing was working on the extension – just lying on a bed with a weight tied around my foot trying to straighten my leg out. Once the leg was straight, that's when we really started the work. Even two minutes with a weight tied around my foot stretching my leg out was agony after my knee had been so stiff for so long. In the year following my microfracture operation, the muscles and the fibres and everything in the knee seemed to have knitted together and tightened up, so this therapy was all about trying to open it all up. As I say, two minutes of it was agony, but we'd often do ten-minute spells a few times a day just to try and relax the knee and get it really opened out.

After a couple of weeks I got into the treatment. It wasn't too bad. I started to feel the benefits of being out there.

Also, once a week I'd see Dr Cugat for a session of blood-spinning. They take your blood, spin it and inject it back into the knee to speed the healing process. It's still quite controversial but a lot more accepted now than it was a few years ago. I felt I had to be bold in my approach. I'd do anything. As long as it was legal, then you could try anything on me if you thought it could possibly make my knee better.

In the month I was out in Terrassa, I picked up some words of Spanish or Catalan, but not nearly enough to hold a conversation. Emili didn't speak much English either, so for some weeks there was a lot of silence during my treatment.

But there was another player being treated at the same time, the Nigerian Christian Obodo, who played for Udinese. He spoke English, so we'd have lunch together. He spoke Spanish too, as well as Italian, so he and Emili understood each other and could have conversations. But I couldn't, and was left out. It was just one of those things. It's not ideal but I was here to try and make my knee better. You just have to get through it.

After I was out there two weeks, another player came out, the Senegalese Salif Diao, who was at Liverpool and Stoke. He obviously spoke English, so now I had someone to have conversations with and work with. When he was there, life became a bit easier for me.

But it was tough. Emili was small but a tough guy. He took

pride in his work. Although it was now the summer, as far as he was concerned we were there to work. Our location in the mountains became part of the physiotherapy. Emili would make us attack the mountain, walking up it as fast as we could for an hour and a half, and then back down again. It sounded like a doddle to me when he told us the first time what we'd be doing, but in practice it was tough, especially to keep your footing. This was all part of Emili's technique of building up the strength around the knee, around all its different surfaces. We used to do that literally every day as well as the work indoors strengthening the knee.

I began to feel confident that I would be able to return back to pre-season in good shape. Knowing that you've given up your whole summer to achieve that felt good. I stayed out in Terrassa for three weeks, then took a brief break when I flew to Dublin for Robbie Keane's wedding, then I flew back out to Barcelona for another week.

Once I'd finished the month of rehab, I was looking forward to putting it to the test. Because when I was out in Barcelona I hadn't played any football. There can't be too many footballers who can say they spent a month in Barcelona but didn't actually play any football!

I got back to Spurs for the start of the pre-season. I was keen to see how my knee felt once I started playing. I was hoping that the work that I'd done would stand me up to get through pre-season with the team, and then take it from there.

For a little while the knee felt OK, but it was just something that I had to put a bit of faith in. Compared to six months before, the knee felt a little bit better because I knew that I'd put good work into it. There hadn't been a miracle cure, but there was noticeable improvement. Just getting my full extension back was significant, something I could only work on while not playing because stretching the knee out does stress it. I had to hope that the improvement would continue through a regular programme of rehab and physiotherapy. I'd still have to do it in my own way.

I started to work with Tottenham's rehab specialist physio, Nathan Gardiner. After an injury, he was the guy you'd work with to get back to fitness. Once you were fit, you would no longer need to work with him, but I started to work with him constantly. Nathan knew his stuff. He was good at sensing when players were not always in the greatest of moods coming back from injury and having to focus on rehab every day. Players want to be on the football pitch. It's a difficult job to get players to do things in the gym that they don't find fun. Good as he was at sensing a player's vibes, there were times when he'd say to people, 'I know your head's not really here today, but let's get this work done.' His sensitive but determined approach really helped.

I worked really closely with Nathan for a good few years, and he was great for me. He never let his level slide once. Every day we got the work done we had to do. He had a work ethic, he loved his job. He took pride in getting people back playing and performing. Though he worked with other people too, I was with him every day, and we developed a good trust. He knew that I knew my body, my knee, better than anyone, so he trusted me when something didn't feel right. He'd drop that exercise and try a new technique. We were forever trying to find new ways to get things done that wouldn't adversely affect the knee.

So most of the 2008/2009 pre-season I spent doing my fitness with him as well as doing some of the training with the team. While they trained on the pitch, I'd often be on the other side of the touchline, doing my own one-on-one work. While the team would go on runs, I'd be in the pool or in the gym. No player really enjoys the pre-season running, but you're there together, you work together and you get through it, and you have that sense of fulfilment at the end of a tough pre-season regime. Missing out on the running, I was also missing out on some of the team togetherness. But the team could see I was working just as hard as they were to get fit, so it still felt as if we were all in it together.

With all these elements I was confident that I could continue playing. I was aware that my knee would probably never be the same again, but at this stage I felt I still had a lot to give.

Going into the season, I think I played all of forty-five minutes of pre-season football. Playing so little football in pre-season wasn't ideal, but I had to look past those pre-season games to the season itself. I was confident that as long as I had done what I had to do working on my own on rehab and fitness during pre-season, I'd go into games and my fitness would come eventually.

Again, not ideal, but I took what I could out of the situation. One thing I really could be thankful for was that I was no longer troubled by my metatarsal. Because I wasn't training every day, it wasn't under the same stress, so the threat of it snapping again seemed to fade away.

But if I was in slightly better shape going into the season than I had been the season before, the rest of team started 2008/2009 just as poorly, with identical consequences in October: yet another upheaval.

SWEET RELIEF

Back in the transfer window at the start of the year, my friend Jermain Defoe had left Tottenham for Portsmouth, where he knew he'd get regular first-team games. He became an instant goal machine for his new side, managed by Harry Redknapp.

I missed him, but that's football.

Just how badly he was missed by the club and fans became dramatically clear that summer when the lethal Berbatov-Keane strike partnership broke up. First, in a surprise move, Robbie was signed by Liverpool. He was an important part of the club and he seemed to have found his home, enjoying his time at the top, and having a great season with Berbatov. But I think it was one of those offers too tempting to turn down. I don't think he necessarily wanted to leave Tottenham, but he had an affiliation with Liverpool, so we didn't begrudge Robbie moving.

And then Manchester United made it very apparent that they wanted Dimitar Berbatov, which completely unsettled him at the start of the new season. So much so, in fact, that the manager only used him once briefly as a sub before he headed

Back in action and winning too! I beat Michael Owen for the ball as Tottenham beat Liverpool 2-1, November 2000.

Glenn Hoddle's assistant John Gorman typically trying to lift my spirits after defeat by Arsenal in the FA Cup semi-final, April 2001. I never took losing in my stride.

Losing the League Cup final to Blackburn Rovers in 2002 was a defeat that nearly crushed my self-belief. My error had given away their winning goal. Was my whole way of playing wrong?

Left. Finessing the ball away from Thierry Henry. More than just North London rivals, we saw each other as our toughest challenges. You couldn't relax for a second when he was on the pitch, but he knew he had a job to beat me.

I may have relished the personal battle against Paul Scholes, but never once did Tottenham beat Manchester United during my career as a senior player. Determined to play and entertain, we could seldom close them down.

I score for England in a friendly against the Portugal of Cristiano Ronaldo, Luis Figo and Rui Costa in February 2004. But four months later against the same opponents, I had to go missing.

No one in an England shirt can escape the media pressure. I face the press at our training camp in Portugal at the Euros of 2004. Little did I know what fate had in store.

Above. I bring the score back to 4-3 against Arsenal in the nine-goal basketball-style defeat that began our upswing back to competing with the Premiership elite under Martin Jol.

Left. Taking the weight off the metatarsal broken at Everton in April 2006, I enjoy as a spectator what looks like a successful run-in to Champions League qualification. But the following month 'Lasagne-gate' would deny us.

Left. White Hart Lane rocks and you just had to be there! Michael Dawson and I celebrate Tottenham's 5-1 thrashing of Arsenal to progress to the 2008 League Cup final.

Below. The moment of victory! Woody and I turn to each other as the whistle blows, with Tottenham beating Chelsea to win the 2008 League Cup final.

Glory at last! Robbie Keane and I share the silverware at Wembley Stadium, February 2008. Some people thought I was finished. I proved them wrong.

Receiving treatment from Tottenham's head physio, Geoff Scott, Stamford Bridge, September 2009. I was spending more time with the physios than my teammates, and it was getting me down.

Above. Into the Champions League at last! We mob our winning goal-scorer, Crouchy, in the crucial victory away at Manchester City, 5 May 2010.

Left. Talking to England manager Fabio Capello. Though not all his methods paid off, I have the greatest respect for a man who put a lot of faith in me. The 2010 World Cup went badly wrong for us both.

Above. My final game on 21 April 2012, against QPR. By then I could no longer perform to the standards I'd set myself and had stopped enjoying my football.

Left. Happier days: on the training ground at Spurs Lodge with Gareth Bale. Team togetherness is what I miss most now I've retired from playing.

off to Old Trafford, with a huge price tag to try to justify. We didn't begrudge him his move either, although the way Berbatov left wasn't ideal. As a club we were obviously trying to hold on to him, yet you had a player that was determined to leave. I felt, OK, let's just get on with it without him if he doesn't want to be there. You don't want players who don't want to be there. There's no point in having a player who's going to be leaving in two weeks just for the first or the second game. You might as well play a player who's committed to the team for the entire season, and who's hungry to play.

Berbatov had just had a great season at Tottenham but was now going to the biggest club in the country. Players come and players go. So the new season started, and we were struggling for goals. We were in games, but lacked the firepower to convert our possession into results.

Back in the summer of 2007 we'd signed Darren Bent, who could score goals, but he didn't really fit the way we played. When he's been at his best, he's had teammates play early balls for him to run onto. He liked the ball early, in behind the defenders. We had players who liked to pass the ball around, and I don't think that suited his game. He's a great finisher, but we weren't playing to his strengths. So although Bent had been a great goalscorer in the League for Charlton, and we knew he could get goals, the way we played meant it just wasn't the same for him.

Both he and the team were finding goals difficult to come

by. Benty was the only recognized striker we had, so every game felt like hard work just to hang in there. When we went a goal down, it was difficult to find the goals to get the draw, never mind the win, and that's not a nice feeling. That was often the feeling once we conceded.

With Darren Bent not benefiting from the Spurs style of play and Defoe, Keane and Berbatov all gone, the club brought the Russian Roman Pavlyuchenko as a last-minute solution to our striker shortage on the final day of the summer 2008 transfer window. But it would have been unrealistic to have expected him to start banging in the goals straight away in a completely different environment to the one that he knew, not just footballing but everything else. It wasn't the easiest for him. He struggled with his English at first, and had an interpreter who he walked around with the whole time. You could see that he was one of those people who didn't take too well to being out of his own country. He was quiet and never really looked that comfortable and happy in England, as if it was a job for him to be here rather than something he really enjoyed. He never really opened up, but he was a nice guy. He learned a few words and was quite funny.

Pavlyuchenko was a goalscorer. Sometimes you didn't see him in games, sometimes his touch could be a bit loose, and often his all-round game let him down. But he was a finisher; he had dynamite in both boots. We saw in training that once he brought the ball onto either foot, and cocked his boot back to shoot, you would say 'Goal!' before he hit it. He kicked a ball that well. Defoe was like that too. Pavlyuchenko was a good player for us. When you're searching for a goal, you knew that you could bring him on and he didn't need to find his way into the game; he would have a shot and score a goal. He wasn't a confidence player either; he could be having a terrible game and still produce two goals.

Pavlyuchenko started a few games as strike partner with Bent, but they didn't really gel. They were both players who liked to play up front on their own. Neither liked to link up with another striker. They were both big men and they both wanted to be in the box. There was no link and nobody dropping back.

And we had other problems at the start of that season.

After the boot camp of his first months in the job, our manager Juande Ramos had become more relaxed and would let the players go out together in pre-season. But his English was only coming on slowly, and he relied upon Gus Poyet, the combative Uruguayan former Spurs midfielder, who had now retired from playing, as his interpreter. To do this job alongside Ramos, Gus had been brought back to the club, but I don't know how well they knew each other. Again, like Santini and Jol four years before, it was a mix you hoped would work, but they didn't always have the same ideas.

You could see that Gus had aspirations to be a manager. He would often try to encourage the team and tell them what to do. More than the manager did, Gus understood what the League was about. Not understanding the Premier League enough was probably Ramos's downfall. In cup-ties he was tactically good, especially when they had two legs: he would learn things from the first game and turn them to our advantage to win the second, and as players we trusted him to set up the right tactics to get results. He also knew about the good teams in the League – Manchester United, Chelsea, Arsenal, Liverpool – and could set up tactically against those opponents. But he didn't know so much about the lesser teams, and we didn't prepare to play them in the same way. I think he thought we could just turn up and blow away other teams like they did in Spain. But every game's tough in this league.

Gus Poyet knew that, and beyond his job as interpreter he tried to prepare us for the League games more fully than the manager did. Contradictions opened up between the two sets of instructions we were getting. But regardless of what we were being told, as players you know the game and you go out there and apply yourselves. It wasn't a lack of effort that accounted for our defeats by Middlesbrough, Sunderland, Villa, Portsmouth, Hull and Stoke. The harder we tried the worse it felt. Sometimes you can work too hard – you're doing a lot of running but is it for the right reasons? We were still playing for the manager, we were still trying to get results, but not only did we lack firepower, we lacked understanding of what we were trying to do on the pitch. That we put up a good performance away at Chelsea for a 0-0 draw and could have actually won the game tells you that we could perform given the right tactical preparation, even without firepower.

Chelsea was my last League game under Ramos; yet again he was saving me for cup-ties and the so-called big-league fixtures. At the start of the season, you want to play the first game, you want to be involved. I travelled with the team but I wasn't playing. I don't even think I was on the bench. I missed playing in the 'lesser' League games. I'd declare myself fit and ready to play but I wasn't picked. I understand that it's the manager's choice. But it wasn't like Ramos was new any more and hadn't seen me play or not known what I could do. So of course I was disappointed, but I got my head down, and hoped that something would materialize in the next few weeks.

What materialized was dramatic.

Saturday, 25 October 2008 was another strange night.

Preparing together for Sunday's home game against Bolton, we were in a hotel in Canary Wharf, and at about 10.30 or 11 p.m. I got a call to my room. As I picked up, I'm thinking, who's calling my room so late in the evening before a game? It was Jermaine Jenas, saying we've got a meeting. I thought it was a joke, so I peeked out the door just to make sure, and I saw a few other heads looking out, thinking, is this for real? So we got in the lift and we knew that it was for real. Something was obviously up and we could all guess by now roughly what, especially as Gus was in the lift as well, and he didn't look too happy. In the meeting the chairman himself came down and said that Ramos and Gus and Marcos Alvarez were leaving and Harry Redknapp would be coming in as manager from tomorrow. That was it; so we went back to our rooms.

Yes, there'd been talk in the days before. But we were surprised at the timing; you don't expect such a big announcement to be made on the night before a game. But we weren't downhearted. There was a bit of excitement, to be honest. It had been a difficult time for us with a manager who was not just foreign but whose style of management was so unfamiliar and not really suited to the day-to-day demands of the English League. We were happy to have an English manager back with us, and I think that most of us appreciated Harry's work for other teams. Every player had seen Harry speaking after games and giving interviews on TV. You got a feel for what he'd be like. We went back to our rooms quite excited. It felt like a load had been lifted off us, and we could get back to basics with someone who knew the League inside out.

The following day Harry came up to the hotel and he was just like we imagined he would be. He told it how it was and motivated the players by saying the right things. On his first day he let us know that we had a great group of players and had no business being where we were in the League – bottom, with only two points out of an available twenty-four. It worked right from the off. We were a different team in that first game, his first in charge, though Clive Allen took the team for the game itself while Harry watched.

Before going to the game on the bus, someone opened up their bag and put a pile of sweets on the coach table and said we don't have to hide these any more. About ten other bags opened up, and there were sweets everywhere. Everyone had sweets in their bag that they'd been hiding from Ramos. At last, we felt that we could be ourselves again.

We went into the Bolton game with a new agenda and played with a freedom we hadn't had in the games before and won comfortably. It felt like the start of something new, and we were a different team. We were free!

THE FEELGOOD REVOLUTION

Three days after Bolton came Harry's first game fully in charge – away against Arsenal. No pressure, then.

As I'd played just three days before, this was a game it was judged I'd better sit out. We were erring on the side of caution in the amount of recovery time we allowed my knee between games. Before declaring myself fit to play, I had to be at a level where I felt that I wasn't going to break down. As I got games under my belt, I felt I'd reach a certain stage of fitness where I'd probably be able to play mid-week, and so it proved on later occasions. But at that stage it was still early in my long rehab, and I wasn't playing regularly.

Though I sat out the Arsenal game, there was no way I was going to miss being there. I went to drive down to the Emirates to go and see the lads before the game, but the roads were blocked off everywhere, and I couldn't get anywhere near to the stadium, where I had a space reserved in the car park. I drove around hoping that I wouldn't be spotted in the traffic by any Arsenal fans, and even contemplated parking my car up and walking there, but a moment's reflection told me that wouldn't be very wise. So I ended up driving back home again, hearing the first half on the radio. I got home at half-time so saw the first-half highlights, including David Bentley's amazing volleyed goal, and the whole of the second half.

What a great game for a neutral to watch, and a great game for us to come back in. Leading up to the game there were a few bits and pieces in the paper where one of the Arsenal players said that even their women could beat us, so that didn't go down well. At 4-2 you could see Arsenal were starting to feel too comfortable and cocky for their own good. They began to dilly-dally on the ball, taking the piss. For our third goal, I think it was Sagna dilly-dallying on the ball; we robbed him, and JJ broke away and scored. You could sense that Arsenal got a bit nervous after that, and in the final seconds, when the ball broke for our Croatian midfielder Luka Modrić to shoot and then Aaron Lennon put the rebound away, what Spurs fans were left in the ground went wild. Don't leave the game early – you never know!

It was a great performance and a great game of football. I was proud of the effort that the lads put in, and we showed great spirit. It felt like we were back on the right path.

Interviewed after the game, Bentley was a happy man, and I was happy for him because it had been a difficult start to his Tottenham career since he'd made his move for a lot of money from Blackburn. He said he felt like he could fly; he felt like Superman. That was Bents; he's a good character.

Some Tottenham fans think that David Bentley has lost sight of the football because he started to believe his own publicity. I think if he hadn't been a footballer, he would have wanted to be a rock star, which is very different to how many footballers think. He doesn't want to be defined just by football; while playing the game, he wants to be doing other things too to make him happy. Having different priorities doesn't mean you're a bad person, but it can detract from your football.

David Bentley is a very outgoing person, very bubbly, and he tells it like it is, which sometimes can go against you. And he's been unlucky. Juande Ramos brought him into the club, then he had some injuries. Harry took over, and sometimes your reputation can precede you. Back then, we were struggling, and while we were in that battle, Harry probably felt we needed a certain type of player in midfield, and not Bentley's type. Though he scored that great goal against Arsenal, he didn't really get a chance afterwards and had nowhere to go.

Though we suffered the occasional setback, like defeats in November by Fulham and Everton, the Redknapp effect saw our renewed confidence and will to win converted into points. We hauled ourselves off the bottom of the table and started to do justice to the talent in the team. It really helped when the manager brought back to the fold our strikers Jermain Defoe and Robbie Keane in the winter transfer window.

Apart from climbing the League, we also were competing in the UEFA Cup and had the Carling League Cup to defend.

In both cup competitions, Harry reversed Ramos's policy. Where I played in the early rounds of both cups under Ramos, where we made good progress because he was such a good cup-tie manager, when Harry came in he tended to rest me in the midweek because he was focused on picking his best team for League games, and I was part of his plans in this campaign, which he prioritized above the others.

So, in the League Cup competition, five months elapsed between my two appearances. I played in the opening round, when we beat Newcastle away. And then, a year after we went there to win it with victory over Chelsea, I was picked for the team when we returned to Wembley to try to retain the League Cup against the challenge of Manchester United.

Going back was a different feeling. You even sensed it was a different feeling with the fans too. Driving to the Chelsea game and then inside the stadium, the atmosphere was unbelievable. You could really feel it. Against Manchester United it was all much less intense. Against Chelsea, the London rivalry makes any game that bit more personal and fuels the determination to fight and win. Man United was a team that had been to many finals, and had been mostly victorious, and their fans are used to being at Wembley, so they don't generate as much atmosphere. But then our fans didn't sound quite as up for it as they had either; perhaps the fact that we'd gone out of the UEFA Cup against Shakhtar Donetsk a few days previously had dampened spirits a little. We were also playing a team we usually struggled against, and if all that wasn't enough to subdue the atmosphere, the game itself wasn't a great spectacle.

Man United fielded a weakened team, with Evans, O'Shea, Gibson and Welbeck, but also in their starting line-up they had Evra, Nani, Ferdinand, Scholes, Tevez and, of course, Cristiano Ronaldo. So it was still a very good team. But so were we. I think they were there for the taking that day, and against anyone other than United I think we would have won the day. We got ourselves in good positions with Lennon twisting Evra inside out and causing all sorts of problems, but we just didn't really believe that we were going to score. If we'd have had that belief, it was a game we'd have won.

But as it was, we had to grind out a 0-0, go into extra time then hope to win on penalties. After all, we'd always found it difficult to beat Man United in open play, so maybe on penalties we could do it. But it wasn't to be. Though the final had nothing like the atmosphere of the year before, and the game itself never really kicked off, nevertheless it was disappointing to be on the losing side.

Straight after the game we went back to the hotel for massage, water, hot tea and ice baths, where three or four players could hop in at one time – not something you ever get used to even when you're baking after a training session in the heat like in Sardinia, where I first encountered them with England in 2004. We didn't have the time to allow ourselves the luxury of feeling sorry for ourselves. We had to prepare for the League game against Middlesbrough three days later.

A good League position was the aim, and we were taking pride in charging up the ladder. As we had given away the first eight games, our goal was to turn around a season that started off so badly that people were even muttering about relegation and see how high we could finish in the League to set us up going into the next season. That was our challenge. We rose to it, beating Middlesbrough 4-0.

For the remainder of the season we showed almost championship-winning form, beating Chelsea and losing only to Blackburn and – them again – Man United.

Any time you go to Old Trafford you know that you're going to have to play very well. We hadn't had a result up there in I don't know how long. But Man United do give you a chance to play, unlike a place like Stoke, where you can struggle to string two passes together because they allow you no time on the ball. With United giving you the chance to play, you need to be confident and composed, you need to keep the ball and you need to have a goal threat. I've seen teams go to Old Trafford and try to play, and they've been nice on the ball and had possession but never really looked like they're going to score. Man United sense a team which they have no real cause to fear and they climb on top of you quickly. In this game we kept the ball well, got ourselves into good positions and were causing them a few problems.

But did we believe we'd score? On twenty-nine minutes, Lennon crossed, Bent controlled it and finished at the post. Finally you go there and you've got something to try to hang on to. Then Modrić scores three minutes later, so you're in dreamland. You're on a high, you're buzzing, you're playing well, you're 2-0 up – and I'd been there before.

It's always a case of half-time coming when you don't really need it and they do. I'm sure their manager, Sir Alex, laid into them, and they came back out in the second half guns blazing. When they come out like that, they can be a hard team to contend with. They'll throw everything into the first fifteen, twenty minutes of the second half, and if you can hold them off, then they might lose a bit of confidence and hope, and get careless so you can pick them off.

But once again, twelve minutes into the second half, when you're getting comfortable you can cope, they get a cheap penalty. For me it was never a penalty; our Brazilian keeper, Gomes, got a good hand on the ball. But that's not the way the referee, Howard Webb, saw it. The moment the penalty was given we felt so hard done by we almost knew we were going to lose the game: you're at Man United, you're up against it as it is, they're coming at you, and then they just get that free ride, that goal, that lift. The crowd sensed that there was a fight-back on, and when Man United are chasing a game and throwing caution to the wind, the crowd do get behind them and roar.

Their next goal came ten minutes later, then a minute later they scored the third, and they were 4-2 up another three minutes later. The Spurs old boy Berbatov got the fifth. Once the second one went in, we were beaten in our own minds. The goals then came thick and fast. Sometimes a game can run away from you and you don't know how or why because it happens so quickly. People talk about experience, and experience counts a lot in football, but sometimes you can do nothing. Look at the AC Milan team who lost to Liverpool in the 2005 Champions League final after being 3-0 up at half-time; you couldn't have a more experienced team. But once the flow of a game goes against you, it can be hard to change. Like with AC Milan, it quickly fell apart for Spurs at Old Trafford. I know we look back and blame the referee but we still conceded five goals!

Though in that game the manager Harry Redknapp and his assistant Joe Jordan would both be screaming instructions from the technical area, as club captain I felt I had responsibility to settle people, to get things focused just when things are teetering on the edge. Often when we conceded a goal, although I'm disappointed, my reaction would be to try and lift everyone, get the team believing that you can still come back. That's something that you always have to be doing as a captain. No matter how difficult you realize it is, you let everyone know that they can still do it. But when it's so quick, as in this game with three goals conceded in four minutes, it's more than difficult. Sometimes you get to feel your way back into a game, but this was just wave upon wave of attacks, and we were struggling, we were getting caught out. The players Man U have on the pitch, they do punish you.

As club captain, with Robbie deputizing on the pitch as team captain when I couldn't play, I felt there were no recurring problems as the leader. The hardest thing for me was when I couldn't get on the training pitch. Training with the rest of the lads, I always felt it was easy for me to lead. When I wasn't around the players, that was the difficult one.

The club has a new training complex now with amazing facilities and it's so big I get lost. But back then Spurs Lodge was quite small and there was no place to hide. With not much window light, in the little gym it was quite dark and dingy. I joked that it probably gave me depression. You don't always realize what effect a certain area can have on you. It wasn't a case of not seeing any players; I saw them every day because the place was too small not to see them, but not for long and not even every day because I would leave Spurs Lodge and go swimming as part of my individual fitness regime. We didn't have our own swimming facilities so nearly every day I'd go off to do my pool work in Repton Park, a gated development of houses and flats with its own Virgin Active Health club.

So even when I was seeing the other players, I was missing out on everything going on on the training pitch, the laughs and the banter. At times I felt a bit alienated, but that's just how it was. It wasn't easy.

I wasn't socializing with other players they way we used to coming up together as apprentices. It works in cycles. The younger players in the first team, the Lennons and the Huddlestones, would socialize together and be tight-knit. Then you've got the slightly older group who maybe have wives, girlfriends and a kid or two, and sometimes as a group they will meet and go to a restaurant.

But I'd split up with my ex so didn't fit into that group with the couples, yet I didn't really want to go out with the young players either. I was over going out casually. The only time I ever went out was with the team. With injuries on top of everything else, it was not a good time for me. I just wanted to do my work and come home. So not only was I not training with the team, but I was not socializing with them outside training either. I never had a problem with any of the players personally, but bit by bit circumstances and my reaction to them almost alienated me a little from the team.

Like I said, though, I'd socialize with the players as a team, having a few drinks when the time was right, on occasions when I've been on a high after a result like when we beat Arsenal 5-1 in the semi-final game. But when we celebrated winning the League Cup, I got carried away. The final was such a relief, such a huge load off my shoulders. It wasn't just my problems with the knee itself but the fact that they were saying that my knee was never going to be good enough for me to continue and that I would soon have to retire. All that pent-up tension was released that night at Faces club in Gant's Hill, Essex, where players and fans had a huge celebration. I overdid it, with pictures of me not looking good appearing in the papers the following day. But the way it was reported wasn't too bad, even though I'd had a row with a bouncer.

A few weeks later I was embarrassed again being pictured looking bleary coming out of the Funky Buddha club in London's West End. By then I'd started my world tour looking for solutions to my knee problem following 2007's microfracture procedure, and the news was not encouraging, so I suppose I was trying to cheer myself up.

The following season, playing more games and with reason to be cautiously optimistic that I had a few years left in me yet despite the knee, it was unusual for me to go out with my teammates for no good reason. A fortnight after the defeat at Old Trafford we played a 0-0 draw at home against Everton, and I don't know why but I went out that particular night to a West End club called Punk, where we sat having a drink. I remember leaving the club, then realized I'd left my phone behind so tried to go back in to get it. And it all went off.

I had an altercation with a bouncer. Obviously I'd had a bit too much to drink but I didn't recognize some of the things he accused me in the media of saying to him. Anyone who knows me will confirm what things I say and what things I don't say, regardless of having a drink. Some of the things I was accused of weren't nice.

Anyway, I was taken down to the police station and put in a cell. The police were good; they were helpful. They understood that it was a nothing situation blown up out of all proportion. They put me in a room for a little while where I waited to come and speak to someone. By this stage I was tired and had a little bit of a sleep. An hour or so later I had to give my version of events and I was let out.

I got home about seven or eight on Sunday morning and had to run the gauntlet of media attention outside my house. The most horrible thing was not having a phone or any way for my mum to get hold of me. Once inside my front door, I just wanted to hide under the bedclothes and not come out again.

But I couldn't hide. I had to deal with it. Even though I was shocked at some of the things the bouncer was saying about me, I wanted to clear my name. I'd put myself in a bad situation. I was disappointed that I'd let myself get into a confrontation, and knew I had to apologize to the club, the manager and the fans for letting myself down like that. And then you just try to move on with your life.

I didn't leave my house for three months afterwards. I was disappointed, I was sad, I was down. It was a bad time and I think the whole incident was a reflection of little things. Dealing with the injury was depressing but had to be done, and almost the worst of it was missing my teammates during the week we're all normally together in training. Because I was hardly ever with them any more, every time I was with my teammates I seemed to have a problem. I just enjoyed being around my teammates having a laugh, and I'd get carried away.

The whole thing affected me, suppressing any desire to go out into company and be friendly because it could so easily backfire when something so simple as just having a good time can end in such a bad way. I more or less stopped going out with my teammates in case I got carried away again in their company which I missed so much with my injury. So even though the fuss surrounding the incident fizzled out, I couldn't let myself forget that I'd been silly to have had too much to drink and get myself into that situation.

But no real harm done. You live and learn, and make sure that nothing like that ever happens again.

UP POPS CROUCHY!

Tottenham finished eighth at the end of the 2008/2009 season, having been bottom with two points in late October. I'd had twenty-four starts in the thirty-eight games of the League season, and had been on the pitch for 61 per cent of it. This was a huge improvement over the four League starts and 8 per cent of playing time under Ramos the previous season.

So I had high hopes of the 2009/2010 season, especially when the manager, Harry Redknapp, reunited little Jermain Defoe with his lanky striking partner from Portsmouth, Peter Crouch, who of course had left Spurs as a trainee with me years before. He'd been doing really well playing around the country, and we joked about me being in exactly the same spot he left me in! I love Crouchy as a character and as a person; he's a good friend of mine, and I was delighted to have him back.

Meanwhile, I had a succession of hamstring and thigh problems as well as the knee that meant I started only half our League games, staying on the pitch for even less time as a percentage.

But if too much of what should have been a peak season for me as an experienced defender, still not quite thirty years old, was spent on the treatment table, the team under Harry continued its progress, starting with a 2-1 home win against Liverpool on the opening day of the season. How good it was to start the season not only with a victory but actually playing!

I felt like I was starting to deal with the knee a bit better, but the muscles were one thing that I was struggling with. I was getting through two or three games and then breaking down, and that's maybe because I hadn't fully recovered from certain games before going into the next one. I was pulling muscles all the time – groin strain, hamstring, hamstring again, thigh.

I always wanted to play. I didn't feel any fatigue or tiredness going into the games; I felt OK, as if I didn't really have a problem. But the muscles said differently. It was difficult because when I broke down I'd be out for two or three weeks. Coming back from the muscle strain, I'd train once and then play as soon as I could. There was no finding my feet back in training and practice games. I think I developed a bit of nervous tension as well sometimes because I didn't really know how my body was going to react. I'd play games hoping rather than knowing that I wasn't going to break down.

Coming back from a muscle strain, I'd go into training at around 10.30 a.m. and straight away would start off on the treatment table with a massage and then I'd do some work on extension, flexion and mobilization of the knees with the support of the physio staff. You always get one, two or three other injured players in there as well, but of course who was in there would change from week to week, while I was there all the time. Rain or shine I was there, and I'm sure the physios, who did a great job, were sick of me. By then I was spending far more time with the physiotherapy staff – Wayne Diesel, Geoff Scott and Danny Murphy (no relation to the player), and the two massage therapists, Joe O'Reilly and Stuart Still – than anyone on the coaching staff. They all knew what needed to be done with me on a day-to-day basis. Coming back from the Barcelona trip, Wayne would be the one working with me because he'd learned a few things abroad, methods that he adopted to work on me and which he passed on to the other physios so they knew what to do.

Thirty-first of October was a mixed day for me. On the one hand, we went to Arsenal with our playmaker, Luka Modrić, and right midfielder, Aaron Lennon, missing, and were well beaten 3-0. I did not have a good game against Robin van Persie.

Being at the Emirates meant I missed the only race which the racehorse I co-owned with my old friend from Bow, Ashley Cole, managed to win, the 7.05 p.m. at Kempton Park. King of Defence was a chestnut gelding bought for us by our agents, Jonathan Barnett and David Manasseh of Stellar Management. I faithfully followed that horse to all its races, and then the one I didn't go to it won! Ashley missed it too, of course. But then he had a 4-0 away win at Bolton with Chelsea, the club he'd left Arsenal for, to console him. I was not really much into horses anyway; it was just a little hobby that I thought might be a bit of fun.

Though Ashley was much more in the limelight than I ever was, it would be wrong to think he was the glamour boy portrayed by the media. I always knew him as a quiet and shy lad, especially as a small player before the age of about fifteen, when he got tougher on the pitch and started to get stuck in.

He married Cheryl Tweedy, a big star in her own right, and a lot of media attention came with that, which I think he will have got used to, though I'm not sure how much he enjoyed it. They became the second footballer and pop singer celebrity couple after David and Victoria Beckham. I think David Beckham had a vision of fame from an early age, while I don't think Ashley was thinking ahead, just living life as it came and letting whatever happened happen. I can understand that. We grew up in the same area, one of those places where you don't expect good things to happen to you. Bow doesn't produce superstars. So everything's new to you, and when you're young, you will make mistakes. Everything happened so suddenly for him, from breaking into the Arsenal team to becoming an England international, and getting so much attention can be tough for a young boy with no preparation for it. I'm sure Ashley never imagined being in the media for things other than football.

Rather than fame, it's the love of the game that makes you want to be a professional footballer. Some players lose sight of that. And once they've played a few first-team games, some footballers start to think about the money. It's dangerous. I've always had different priorities. As long as I was happy with my football and in my surroundings, that was the main thing. Luckily for the game, and contrary to what many people might think, for footballers to focus on fame and money rather than football is quite rare.

A game I was forced to watch rather than play in because of my hamstring was the amazing 9-1 over Wigan on 22 November, when we were only 1-0 up at half-time, thanks to Crouchy, with our opponents looking well capable of a comeback. But in the second half Defoe was on fire. Everything he hit went in the back of the net, and he ended up with five goals.

I was out until brought on as a sub in a 0-0 Boxing Day draw with Fulham. That was the time when, as club and team captains, Robbie Keane and I got involved in a difference of opinion with the manager that landed Robbie in hot water. Harry always said that players shouldn't have a drink in the season, with no exceptions, so he didn't want the team to have a Christmas party. But the team always wanted one and came to me or Robbie, saying they didn't see why we couldn't – every team has a Christmas party. My view is that, if it's at the right time, there's nothing wrong with it. And that is despite the fact that, after my embarrassments overdoing it with teammates the two previous seasons, I would be going very easy myself if even having a drink at all. Because Harry was making it a big issue when no other team had a problem with Christmas parties, a lot of the players felt we were being highlighted, and almost punished, which made it an even bigger problem for us.

Some of the younger boys liked to get together as a group and go out when the time was right. The fact that it was highlighted in the press that we weren't allowed out made people take pictures if they saw players out enjoying themselves. Even the older players weren't treated as adults: players who'd meet up with their partners and go for a meal with a drink or two would often be asked, 'What are you doing out?' Crouchy and Woody had some pictures taken of them; they were doing nothing wrong – they were having a dance or something – but the pictures were made out to look like they were up to no good. Feeling under that kind of scrutiny didn't help.

Unlike in the era when Harry played, when drink was a big part of football culture and I'm told might partly account for why his old club, West Ham, underachieved despite being full of World Cup winners, with the number of games we've got now we just couldn't do it. Yes, you'd get some players who would let their hair down at the weekend after a game. When I was coming through I played with Teddy Sheringham, and he was a player who after a game would have to unwind with a few drinks. That was what he found worked best for him – and he was never injured and played until he was forty-two. But that old-school football culture of mid-week drinking and going to the pub after training is not in football any more. Players will get together and have a drink when the time is right. Obviously the main thing is not to abuse it. A drink every so often is not going to affect you.

So, I understood where Harry was coming from, especially with my own recent troubles getting carried away over a few drinks with my teammates. At the same time, I felt sorry for the lads being spied on and photographed and challenged every time they went out to have a perfectly innocent social time, whether at a restaurant, bar or club. So before Christmas 2008 I had to go to speak to Harry. I said I understood that we didn't need the Christmas party, and I'd rather not have the stress of going out and maybe getting too relaxed and ending up in trouble, but I felt that, if we're going to have one then, as club captain, I've got to be there. If we can't have one, we can't have one, but the players still had the day off and would maybe go out and do their own thing; it was a situation where you didn't want the players to rebel.

So we agreed that as long as there was no trouble we could go ahead, and that's what happened. But a year later, in the week or so before Christmas 2009, the problem arose when Robbie organized a team trip to Dublin, where we celebrated Christmas early because of how the fixtures were scheduled. Thinking we'd just gone on a golfing trip, the manager said something in the press about banning Christmas parties but didn't tell us, and by then it was too late: we'd had the Christmas party and got it out of the way. When the press found out that we'd had a Christmas celebration it looked bad. It looked as if we'd gone behind his back and mocked his authority, and we were fined and disciplined.

But in the event, the time was right and there were no problems. Apart from a freak home defeat to Wolves, the results were good in that Christmas period and don't reflect anything to do with a group festive celebration. We had great times when the group was together, bonding us tighter as football team. All chat reverts to football. We'd often find ourselves in a huddle talking about what we needed to do on the pitch. It was all great for team spirit.

I don't think we came together as a group often enough for meals and so on, but that's probably because I was not training with the lads. Staying inside that team bond when I wasn't training with the players and then trying to make that connection off the pitch without getting carried away was difficult for me. After I'd been in trouble once I shied away from being out with the team.

Aside from Crouchy and Jermain Defoe, another Tottenham old boy who Harry Redknapp signed from Portsmouth was the French defender Younès Kaboul, who returned in the January 2010 transfer window. Younès had originally joined the club at a young age. He had the size, he had the speed, he had a powerful shot on him and loved to come out of defence and have a go at goal from thirty or forty yards. He had all the ingredients except for his concentration.

I've often seen players with all the attributes apart from

what's going on in their heads. To correct the tendency to lose concentration, I think players need to mature. They need to play and learn as they go along. Younès was a player who liked to take a few risks at first. Sometimes he'd get caught on the ball doing too much, and that's something that he learned to avoid. He's matured as a player, he's got to the right age. Now, although he still gets forward because he's such a good athlete, hard to catch once he has the ball at his feet, he's doing it less and less but doing it at the right times. As a player that's how you mature, knowing when to do it and when not to.

It would have helped him going to Portsmouth and playing with an experienced group of players down there like Sol Campbell and Sylvain Distin. Playing every week would have brought him on, as he learned about the Premiership week in week out.

When he come back he played right-back quite a few times towards the end of the season, with me and Dawson at centre-back. I like Younès at right-back. For one thing, he had size, and if any crosses came into the box he'd pick up a good position because naturally he was a centre-half and he'd get his head on it. Also, being a good athlete, that position suited him at the time because as a young boy he had energy to burn and could get up and down the right side. When you have energy to burn and so much to give, you want to get involved and often run to places you don't need to, keen to set up goals, and that can be a problem at centre-back.

So with Younès, we felt that we had a good foundation going into the run-in, chasing that Champions League-qualifying fourth spot.

At the back end of that season we had a tough run-in, with games against Arsenal, Chelsea and both Manchester clubs in the last six fixtures, and people were beginning to write off our chances. Though I sat out our victory over Chelsea, I played in our 2-1 North London derby win, another evening game crowned by a spectacular volleyed goal. Ten minutes in, we had Arsenal under pressure, but their keeper, Almunia, managed to parry the ball well out of the area. On the full volley, our young left-back, Danny Rose, didn't do the obvious thing and dink it back into the mixer, but unleashed a forty-yard shot which swerved over everyone's heads and smacked into the back of the net. It was a moment of inspiration as well as world-class technique, and was fully the equal of David Bentley's goal at the Emirates eighteen months before. Gareth Bale had a superb game, tormenting Arsenal throughout and scoring our second goal just after half-time. Shortly before full-time, Nicklas Bendtner pulled one back for them, but it was too little, too late. Arsenal's title hopes ended that night, while we advanced towards Champions League qualification.

Though we lost at Old Trafford we gave them a game till the end. Then the big one up at Man City; win this, and we would qualify for the Champions League ahead of them in fourth place. So it was make or break. Going into the game on good form obviously breeds confidence, and we were confident that we could get a result. We also had a good record up there, but by now Man City were assembling a team, with Petrov, Adebayor, Tevez and Barry, which could compete for titles. They were on their way to competing for titles and we were on our way to entering the Champions League; our paths crossed, and it was a shoot-out.

Looking at players like Tevez, we obviously respected their talents and their brilliance, but we felt like we'd been in this together for a little while, had been through the frustration and heartbreak of just failing to make the top four, and it was a game that we wanted to win badly. We had the team spirit, and I think that's what came through on the night.

It was a perfect game for us. It's not too many times Tottenham can go away from home and win 1-0. It was a mature performance. The first half Man City started off quite brightly and had a few chances, but we got into the game and created the better ones. I think Crouchy hit the post, I had a goal disallowed, and Gareth Bale had a left-foot shot that whiskered past the post. By half-time we felt we were the better team. You just hope that you go out there for the second half and can do it again. Sure enough, Crouchy repaid his transfer fee by popping up with a goal that sealed it for us.

For once losing the last game of the season – against Burnley – didn't matter. We were where we'd been trying to get back to for years: among the European elite.

THE ENGLAND HAIR-SHIRT

It was among the global elite where I found myself next: the 2010 World Cup.

I was twenty-nine, turning thirty that October, and injury problems were keeping me out of more and more games. When I was invited to the England training camp, I tried not to think about it too much but knew it was probably my last chance of getting anywhere near an international trophy. I'd not played for the national team for a good few years, so I was very lucky to be asked at all.

Would this England training camp be a starting point again for me as an international? I wasn't sure. With the knee I was always trying to find solutions to help me to play more games, and the way I'd finished the season I was optimistic. So I went into the squad feeling pretty good about myself.

People say to take the tournament game by game, and it was like that for me. I was just going to take it as it came. I wasn't sure what was round the corner with my knee. I tried to look after it and keep going with it. Would it be my last tournament? Probably yes, but at the time my mind was fixed on going out there, trying to do a job, trying to perform well to help the team.

This would my first experience of the new England manager, Fabio Capello. He'd enquired about me in recent years, but I never felt the time was right. I never felt I'd put a run of games together for my club where I felt confident enough to go away with England knowing that I'm going to get through a tournament without breaking down. I'd told him at the time that I didn't feel fit enough to join in with England. I didn't want to go as a squad member and then have to pull out with injury. I thought it was right to just try and concentrate on getting in as many games as I could for Tottenham.

But the World Cup came along, and at the time I felt like I was in good shape to go. I'd read in the papers that Capello had compared me to the likes of Paolo Maldini. I'd watched Maldini on Channel 4 Serie A football throughout the '90s, and he is one of the most complete players as full-back or centre-half I've ever seen. I was very flattered, so when Capello called me up for the 2010 World Cup squad, I felt he had huge faith in my ability as a player and I wanted to repay him by proving him right.

Before meeting Capello for the first time, I'd obviously heard a lot about him from teammates who had played in his squads: Lennon, Defoe, Jenas and Dawson. I'd often ask them the question, what's he like? The feedback was that he was tough. He'd gone in there and shaken the place up with his rules. Lots of the things that I'd known previously with Sven-Göran Eriksson and Steve McClaren had gone out of the window, mainly the relaxed camp. Things had toughened up a lot. And they were also less fun.

Before I joined up with the squad, I'd heard that the manager had been shouting at the players around the hotel, and I'd built up such a picture of Fabio Capello in my head that it was a surprise and a relief to find that he was actually a lot softer than I'd imagined. He wasn't a monster, and I liked him. We had good conversations, and I grew to have a lot of respect for him. It can't have been easy for him with me coming into the team with my style of training, yet he tried to make it as comfortable as possible for me. Recalling how it had been for me with Ramos, I didn't think he'd be so accepting of the fact that I didn't train.

Just before the World Cup tournament, that May the squad of twenty-nine potential England picks went to Capello's favourite altitude training camp in Irdning, Austria. That was a little bit boring for the lads. We went out to train, and though my knee meant I only took part in a few of them, some of our sessions were quite intense, which was fine, but there was nothing else to do. Fabio Capello had stated that there would be no wives or girlfriends allowed, and the ten days there felt a bit like being at boot camp – a boot camp in a five-star hotel.

At the Hotel Schloss Pichlarn, the England squad and staff had their own section. Though Capello's rule had been that we couldn't start dinner until everyone had turned up, it had been relaxed by the time I came in. Other rules hadn't. Sometimes you get bored in the hotel, and players would have friends who'd bring DVDs round for the lads to watch. That stopped. Some players liked to get a haircut in their hotel room. That stopped too. It seemed petty to be complaining about these rules, but we never could work out the problems they were invented to solve. I think certain things got lost in translation. Though you could see he was trying his hardest, Capello's English still wasn't great. He could communicate with us, but you could see that it wasn't easy for him.

The players appreciated Capello as a manager, but the general feeling was that sometimes you can get a foreign manager who comes and tries to change everything without really knowing the style and the character of the English. That doesn't mean drinking, that doesn't mean getting into trouble: it means team spirit. As I could confirm from when Juande Ramos managed Tottenham, sometimes people from different countries come in with philosophies that are so foreign to what we're used to that they create friction. While I'm all for learning and new experiences, I think the feeling about Capello was that we'd never in our lives had his kind of approach before, and some of his demands were a bit petty.

Having been away for ten days in Austria with absolutely nothing to do, by the time the World Cup itself came along a month later in South Africa, I think the players were a little bit bored and drained. Though our base in South Africa was quite isolated, when you're out there in the World Cup you've got a job to do, and I didn't have a problem with the isolation. But at the time I felt that the Austria trip could have been a little bit more relaxed and fun to bring the team together and galvanize our spirit going into the tournament.

But from the personal point of view, from my time working with him I've only got good things to say about Fabio Capello.

Halfway through the training camp we had a break back home to play a friendly at Wembley against Mexico, which we won 3-1. Later, in South Africa, we played a friendly against a local team, and in both games the warm-ups were quite intense. I felt heavy-legged. I think the other lads were fine, but because I only did a couple of training sessions, the intensity of it took it out of my legs. I'm sure the other lads found the intensity of the training quite tough too, but I could feel my legs were really tired. I put that down to the fact that I wasn't as fit as everyone else in the first place.

The first game of the tournament for England was against the USA. I went into the game feeling fine. I'd made a couple of changes. Before the game I decided to do my own warm-up away from the team. But I didn't have the cycling shorts that I'd been wearing for years, which made my thighs and muscles feel warmer, more stable and more compact. I'd asked the England kit staff for the kind I usually wore, which I knew and trusted, but there was a bit of a mix-up. There were some cycling shorts provided on match day, but not the kind I'd asked for. I didn't like them so I decided to go without. As well as my decision to warm up on my own, I still think about that decision to shed the shorts because of what happened next.

Just three minutes into the game, stretching a little bit, I reached for a header. I felt something go in my groin. My first reaction was: please, no, it can't be happening. I tried to keep moving, and Gerrard scored our goal within seconds.

I said to John Terry next to me, 'I think I've done my groin,' and I remember him shouting to the side, but I tried not to look. I'd gone into denial about it; in my mind, this wasn't happening. I didn't want to look over to the coaches and I didn't want to tell them anything. But they were asking, 'How is it?' so I said, 'Let me see.'

I thought I might be able to run it off – maybe it was just a little bit of tissue, the muscle fibres stretched a little bit. Luckily I didn't really get tested because I really couldn't bring myself to come off the pitch during the first half. Pride meant I couldn't just walk off the pitch. I thought, if I'm going to come off, it's going to have to get to the stage where I can't walk and they'll have to take me off on a stretcher. Otherwise, I'll struggle through to half-time and assess the situation then.

I felt I'd let people down. I'm sure there were question marks over my selection because of my injuries, but the manager had put his faith in me by picking me. So I particularly felt I'd let Fabio Capello down.

Somehow I managed to struggle through to half-time. While Capello was talking to the team, for me even getting up onto the bed for the doc and the physio, Gary Lewin, to assess the injury, was hard work. And when they opened out my groin I felt searing pain. We all knew at once that I couldn't go back out. They iced it, but as half-time wore on it felt worse and worse.

The next thing was to have a scan in the morning, and we had to wait until then to know the damage: it was a grade-two tear, which, they said, could take three weeks to heal. That wasn't great to hear, but Capello and his ever-present right-hand man, Italo Galbiati, said they knew someone who might be able to help heal the injury more quickly, a guy who works in Italy with a lot of big clubs and players. I was obviously up for giving it a try. David Beckham told me that, while he was in Italy playing for AC Milan, he saw Gennaro Gattuso have this method of healing, and he was almost in tears it was so intense. Gattuso in tears?! It was a scary thought.

I got to learn how the treatment felt first-hand. I'd work three times a day with the guy who applied electro pads to different parts of my body, sometimes my stomach, sometimes my sides and thighs, and they'd turn it up to as much as I could handle. The pain was excruciating. It could well have qualified as torture. The pads on my stomach would cramp me up and keel me over, and I'd have to try and straighten out and stand up and take it. I did three sessions of thirty minutes to an hour every day, often starting at 10 a.m. and finishing at 10 p.m. I dreaded going to every single session because of the pain. But I was determined to get through it, to try to get myself back to fitness as soon as possible and try to do what I set out to do, which was prove my worth to the squad.

The treatment worked. Within ten days I managed to return to the squad and was back, fit for selection for the Germany game. By then it was a bit of a gamble to throw me straight back into the starting line-up, so I found myself on the bench.

Matthew Upson had partnered John Terry as centre-back in the game before, against Slovenia, so the manager decided to stick with that team, which included Defoe, who'd scored in that game. Although disappointed, I couldn't argue with that decision. But I felt that I would have been better suited to counter the pace of the German team; between Terry and Upson we didn't really have much pace.

So I sat on the bench and watched a very good German side destroy us 4 1.

After the defeat, which knocked us out of the World Cup, Capello spoke in the dressing room. What he said I can't remember. It falls on deaf ears at the time; the game's finished, the tournament's over, the mood's low. Most people are just sitting there in a kind of trance thinking about the fact that they haven't performed. We have to go back to our country and face our people, face our fans, knowing that we've let them down. There wasn't too much said by anyone in the changing room.

Obviously, we were very disappointed that we'd not got into our stride and played well in the entire tournament. We couldn't argue with the judgement back home that we hadn't performed. We were disappointed to let down the country, the nation, the manager. It was almost a sense of embarrassment.

Throughout the tournament we hadn't performed, so we could already feel going into the Germany game that we were underachieving. Though we'd had three group games and not played particularly well, you often look back at the finalists' group games and they often didn't perform that well And sometimes you get teams who ease through their group, scoring plenty of goals, and they lose the first round of the knockouts. So the tournament's about trying to improve. You start off slowly but you want to see progress in your play. You want to peak at the right time.

We scraped through the group so we entered the Germany game hoping to kick-start the tournament at that point and go from strength to strength. But nothing had changed from the group games; we had not got going at all.

We went home with our tails between our legs, and I don't think too many players were looking forward to getting off the plane back in England to the reception we were going to receive. You hope to go away and come back as heroes, or at least you want to come back knowing that you've given your all, and the fans are proud of you, like the England teams of 1990 and 1996, which, though they didn't win the tournaments, galvanized the fans. The country was behind them and appreciated their efforts.

I didn't have that feeling coming back. When the plane landed back in England, we almost didn't want the doors to open. We just wanted to stay in there nice and safe for as long as possible.

Every England game is scrutinized. There was a lot of criticism that England never looked comfortable on the ball. Players, who for their clubs looked perfectly comfortable on the ball, for some reason, when it came to the national side, struggled with basic skills like trapping and passing. It was true. We were all quality players. There was no technical reason why we could perform so well for our clubs and then, when we put on the England kit, it doesn't happen. I can only say it's maybe the weight of the England shirt, the weight of expectancy from the media, from the fans. It weighs heavy on some players.

When you meet up with England you're always aware of what's going on in the media. You try to block it out as much as you can, try not to pick up the papers, try to stay away from the football channels. But deep down inside we all know there's a lot of coverage any time the team gets together. It's a million-dollar question why the team hasn't done well. We've had the players to go there and perform on a much higher level and get a lot further in competition. I think it's the pressure. When you're a team, you need to all come together and be on the same page. That probably hasn't been the case enough with the England teams I've played in.

You only need a few players not performing and it can affect the whole team. Once that nervousness enters the team with one or two players, it spreads. That's something I noticed playing with England: you felt you were waiting for things to go wrong. We were expecting criticism. There was no freedom when we played; we were almost walking on eggshells. It wasn't the way that the players are used to playing with their clubs. They play with a freedom and expression, but it just didn't happen when we put on an England shirt.

My three minutes against the USA was the last time I put on the England shirt. Had I worn the shorts, warmed up with the rest of the team, not got injured against the USA and been fully fit and picked to start against Germany, could things have been different? Maybe. But maybe not different enough to change the outcome of what was a very one-sided game against Germany.

I had to put the boredom of Austria, the agony of Italy and the disappointment and embarrassment of South Africa behind me and look forward to what promised to be an exciting season with Tottenham: in the Champions League at last.

'I'LL GIVE IT A GO'

Of all the Spurs teams I played in, the generation of the 2010/2011 season was probably the most exciting. Training sessions buzzed with one-touch link-up play at pace – I'd be amazed at what we could do. On the pitch too, Luka Modrić, his fellow Croat Niko Kranjčar, the South African arriving in the winter transfer window Steve Pienaar and the Dutchman Rafael van der Vaart played some great football. Niko was technically perhaps even better than Luka; he could hit a ball and had some close skills too. It was a pity that Pienaar never really felt at home in the team. He never really got a run in the side and didn't settle.

But all in all, they were exciting times.

Including the right-back Vedran Ćorluka, our three Croatian players had a special bond. All spoke good English. I think Niko had lived in America in his early years and spoke better English than some of the English players. Luka was a quiet lad when he first came in, but his English was OK, and Ćorluka's was good as well. They were good lads and mixed in well with the team. But they had a real closeness together. We used to say that Luka and Vedran Ćorluka used to sleep in the same beds on away trips. They had their own rooms but slept in each other's rooms because they were never apart from each other. It was good for the team when the foreign players felt comfortable within the team because they had someone from their own country who shared their language and culture. The three of them had a real passion for their country; they loved going away and playing for the Croatian national side. I could feel the difference between them and the English when the England team got together. With England it seldom felt quite right.

Just before the summer transfer window closed we'd signed from Real Madrid their unsettled player Rafa van der Vaart. This last-minute transfer coup came as a big surprise for everyone, but he gave the place a major lift. A player with great quality and experience playing for top sides in massive tournaments, Rafa was a player we were delighted to have on board. He settled in easily. He enjoyed London and enjoyed his football at Tottenham. We were a team that suited his style of play, and he quickly developed a good understanding with Crouchy, playing off him. Crouchy would assist by holding the ball up for him as he made his way into the box or provided the knock-downs for Rafa to slot home. They struck up a good relationship with his timing of his runs. Rafa had quality in his left foot, and could produce a moment of magic going forward.

But of all the players who made an impact that season, it was Gareth Bale who became a sensational household name. He'd come to Tottenham from Southampton aged only seventeen but with a big price tag; even then, he'd been identified as a player with huge talent and potential. But he struggled with injury and doubts about what was his best position: left-back or left-midfielder? He also seemed to be cursed: he played a record-breaking unbroken run of twenty-four League games for Spurs without once being on the winning side. You have to look at individual performances throughout the run where we didn't win a game. You can never say it's down to one Jonah player. I'm sure Gareth had plenty of great performances in there. One man can never do it on his own, and it works the other way: you can't go that number of games without a win and blame it on one player, the team albatross. It's down to the team, and all Gareth had to do was concentrate on performing well when he played.

I had no doubt he was going to be a top player. It was just what position he was going to make his own that was the question, because he could play in both. If he was going to commit to left-back he needed a bit of work. He was a young player who needed to learn the defensive side of the game a little bit. He already had the ability to fly down the left wing and help out in attack. Mastering the defensive side of his game would come.

Or was he going to play midfield? If so, he had to supply

crosses into the box and pin back the full-back, causing opponents problems in the same way that Aaron Lennon was doing
on the right of the pitch. Gareth had to make a difference, once
he'd sorted out his injuries and best position. There aren't too
many left-footed players around let alone players of Gareth's
ability. I had no doubt that he was going to be a top player.
And that season he proved it to the world.

For me personally, though, the 2010/2011 season was a non-
event.

I'd come back from the World Cup, which had ended for
me after only three minutes of effective play thanks to groin
strain in the game against the USA. At the beginning of this
season, my groin was still not feeling right. Not the torn right
side, though, but the left. While I was doing my rehab for my
injured right groin, I started to feel a little bit of pain very high
up on my left side, almost up against the bone. It was a dull
ache if I stretched the groin. While doing rehab on my right
side, I wasn't thinking too much about my left side aching. It
wasn't a problem I saw stopping me from playing.

I went back to the pre-season and then played in the home
leg of the Champions League qualifying round against the
Swiss side BSC Young Boys, and then I played against Werder
Bremen away. I could still feel the groin. By now it was aggra-
vating me but not necessarily stopping me from playing. So
I just kept going. But the following game, an away win at
Fulham just after my thirtieth birthday, I stretched for a ball

and felt the groin go, as if I'd pulled the muscle away from the bone.

I didn't know how bad it was at the time, but this injury kept me out for seven months. Doing my work with Nathan Gardiner on my own outside the training ground, I kept getting back to a certain level of rehab, but it continued to aggravate me. We went through lots of different things. The initial injury was in the groin, but when I came back after six weeks I was getting pain higher up in my stomach.

I ended up having a hernia operation out in Munich, Germany. The female surgeon, Ulrike Muschaweck, who performed the operation, had done a few that season for some of the other players.

I left within hours of the operation and flew back the same day. The lads who'd had the operation before me said that afterwards they were in agony walking through the airport. I got up off the plane after the operation and could barely stand. With the pain in my abdomen, I felt physically sick and couldn't stand up straight. I shuffled through the airport like an eighty-year-old.

They said that after this operation I'd be back training within seven to ten days. At this point I couldn't see how, but the players who'd had the operation before me had got back into training pretty quickly, so I was hopeful. But I still continued to get a pain. The stomach pain had gone, but this pain high up on the bone was still causing me a problem when I stretched.

Three months after the operation and after a day or two of training, I was on the bench for the second leg of the Champions League tie against AC Milan, and in the warm-up at half-time I kicked the ball and felt something go again. You can imagine how I felt. I didn't want to say anything to the manager. I just hoped that I could sit there and not be used. But obviously I had to tell them that I felt something go in my groin again so I wasn't able to come on if needed.

At this point I didn't know when I was going to be back and ready. It was an ongoing problem. Every day I would go in and do my work but didn't really want to be around the place too much. I think all injured players feel the same, especially when you're out for long stretches: you feel like a liability, so you want to do your work then disappear.

The thought of what I would do after my playing career was increasingly in the back of my mind as I got older, but this wasn't an injury I thought I'd never come back from. It wasn't the knee but a soft-tissue problem that we were struggling to find a way of fixing. It never crossed my mind that I wouldn't play again. What was on my mind was the question of what was going to get me over this injury.

It took me seven months in total to finally shake this injury off. I started to feel a little bit better towards the end of the season and I actually travelled to the Liverpool game on 15 May 2011, to be with the team at the request of the manager. I'd trained a few times leading up to that week after seven months out but I was not expecting, nor feeling ready, to play.

In the changing room an hour and a half before the game the manager asked me if I could play.

'Harry,' I said, 'I don't think I can do it. I don't feel confident enough to get through the game. I'd be more disappointed if we won 2-0 and I scored both goals but then had to come off through injury than anything else. If I have to come off the pitch injured again two games from the end of the season when I've been out for seven months, that's going to kill me. I can't come back and then break down again after all that time.'

Harry considered this, then said, 'We could do with you if you can.'

The next thing I know, I'm saying, 'I'll give it a go.'

But I had no confidence in getting through the game. I was out there fingers crossed.

Just the fact that I was out there I think gave the team a lift. More than the fact that I played well, I was happy that I contributed to the team winning and I was even happier to have come through the game with no repercussions.

Having to spend so much of not just that season but several previously sitting out games and watching rather than playing, there were times where I'd see that when I was playing we were a lot tougher to beat than when I wasn't. Every player's aware of what results you're getting when you play, and I was aware that we won a lot more games than we lost when I was playing.

That's not down to me as a player who scores goals but as someone who maybe makes everyone else play a bit better. I felt going into games that it wasn't always about my performance but my presence lifting the people around me: the defender next to me played better, the full-backs played well. Maybe the crowd had a lift too, and that lifted the players.

That's what gets you out there at times when you're not feeling great: you're trying to lift the team. I finished off the season at home to Birmingham and came through that game all right too.

Although it was not great timing to be fit only at the end of the season, it was reassuring in a way. Hopefully I would not be going into the next season with the same problems as I had before.

THE BITTER END?

That summer wasn't ideal for Tottenham. Just as with Berbatov a few years back, we weren't sure whether Luka Modrić was coming or going. Chelsea had offered £40 million for him, and Luka's mind was elsewhere. So for the first two games of the season, the playmaker of the team was there but of no use to us.

I missed the first two games too, and we were hammered by both Manchester United and City.

But just before the transfer window closed, in came my old schoolboy rival Scotty Parker from West Ham, and, on loan from Man City, Emmanuel Adebayor.

By the time the third game came along we felt ready. I was back from injury, Scotty and Adebayor had come into the side, so going into the Wolves game our team felt strong; we felt comfortable with each other and ready to start the season from here and fly up the League. We quickly went on a good run of results, beating Wolves, Liverpool, Wigan and Arsenal in succession.

I was not sure whether I was going to pull up with more

muscle injuries, but I always said that, with four or five games under my belt, I could start to really get myself going and rather than just be there trying to stabilize the team, I could focus on my own form.

Though I felt much better than I had the previous season with the groin problem, I was a marked man as a result. Knowing that I wasn't training, opposing strikers thought they could tire me out by continuously working me down the channels, trying to make me run, twist and turn. Sure enough, four days after my thirty-first birthday, away at Newcastle, where we were held to a 2-2 draw, on the half-hour I made a turn and a run and I felt something go in the groin.

I came back from that two weeks later and I was determined not to have any more of these injuries. All was going well, with no more injuries in competitive play. At a training session that Christmas I was feeling good, which was rare, and if anything I was too excited, running around a bit too much. A cross came in, our young reserve keeper, Oscar Jansson, came out, I'd got my eye on the ball, and we collided. I went down with all my weight on the outside of my left knee, and the keeper fell down on top of me. It was a complete accident.

There was a lot of pain which I'd never really had before. In games my knee never really hurt apart from sometimes being shaken up a bit in a slide tackle, but nothing that wouldn't ease away a few minutes later. But this blow to my knee took it to a place where it hadn't been before. The knee swelled up quickly, and by the following day it was huge. We tried to drain it with a syringe and took out 60 or 70 ml of fluid; it kept refilling. But even when the fluid was out, the knee didn't feel right.

After I'd been out a month or so with the knee, it still didn't feel right but I was ready to give it a go. I loved throwing myself in if I thought I could help, and the next game back was away at Manchester City. They were the League leaders, while we were lying third, only five points behind; win this, and we were in with a serious shout of the Championship.

It was a day when we just didn't have the luck. We did brilliantly to come back from 2-0 down and nearly had a winner, with Jermain just failing to poke it home. Mario Balotelli had come off the bench for City to try to win them the game, and had already seen yellow for fouling Benoît Assou-Ekotto when four minutes later he stamped on Scotty Parker. Had the referee seen what many of the players had and everyone watching on TV, then I doubt Balotelli would have stayed on the pitch. But stay on he did, and four minutes into added time he was advancing on our goal.

I felt certain that he would score and I had to make a challenge. With hindsight I should have let the keeper make a save; I should have left Balotelli with the task of having to beat Brad Friedel. I don't often make rash decisions, but this was rash, a poor challenge. My moment of rashness boiled down to the fact that I wasn't 100 per cent, was a yard or two in the wrong place, I was over-stretching and I couldn't make the tackle.

Yes, it was a penalty, and, as cool as you like, Balotelli slotted it home. A minute later the final whistle blew.

This was more than a disappointing end to the game for me. As I came off, I saw the cameras coming to me, and I tried to crash out. I was exhausted and devastated, and I couldn't put any weight on my left knee.

Limping down the tunnel, I didn't even get into the changing room; straight away I was pulled in for drug-testing. This was the last thing I needed. I was whisked into a side room with two Man City players who were obviously delighted with their last-gasp win. I don't think I said a word. We'd got ourselves back in the game, but then I'd given away the penalty that cost the team. And now this. I felt things couldn't get any worse.

Any player hates getting drug-tested because after a game you're dehydrated. Sometimes it can take you hours to pee for their sample. I sat in there for an hour or so. I didn't even get a chance to see my teammates until I got on the bus. Everyone was dressed and ready and on the team bus waiting for me. It was a weird end to a bad day.

Though we recovered our momentum as a winning team, for me that defeat at Manchester City was a turning point. Ever since I'd taken that whack in training I couldn't do what I wanted to do. I no longer had that extra percentage that I needed to make a difference. I was struggling. Up until then, we hadn't lost with me in the team. But now we had, and the record had gone. After the City game I started to question whether the knee would hold out. As always, though, my aim was to get through to the end of the season and then look at the picture again.

I played the next three games. We beat Wigan, drew 0-0 away at Liverpool and beat Newcastle 5-0. That evening, arriving at Tottenham on a six-month contract from Everton, Louis Saha was unstoppable in strike partnership with Adebayor. I was excited by Saha. I'd obviously played against him, and on his day he was up there with the best of them. He'd struggled with injury so I could relate to him; he had a knee problem as well. We'd often speak about our situations and try to help each other with little tips. He had to miss days of training as well, but at the same time was trying to do as much as he could until the end of the season to secure a longer contract at Tottenham. I think that made it difficult for him because he felt he had to try and train more and give more than he probably wanted to or could at that stage. But when he played he still had quality to give. He was a great finisher with both feet; in training we weren't sure which foot he kicked with, he just kicked so easily with both. He gave us a bit of a lift.

With Saha scoring goals, the results for Tottenham were still there. But any player knows within himself how he's moving, and inside I knew that I was even more restricted than ever. I was lucky that so far I was good enough to get away with it. But I knew. And at the Emirates I got found out.

We went into the game feeling good off the back of the Newcastle win and started off well, going into a quick 2-0 lead.

Even so, Arsenal still had a lot of possession. Bacary Sagna would just keep bombing on down the right as their free man and outlet. He was constantly getting to the byline or level with the eighteen-yard box and crossing balls or playing on from there. So even though we were 2-0 up we still felt like there was work to be done. We still had to figure out how to get a proper foothold in the game.

Soon after our second, against the run of play, we seemed to be clear in on goal for a third. But it didn't go in, and from that point Arsenal appeared to become a lot more confident and were really pushing. We were on the back foot and never seemed able to break out of our area after that. We were trapped on the edge of our box and found ourselves dropping deeper and deeper.

When Arsenal do play they can be difficult because, if you go chasing, they will play around you. So rather than opening up, we felt that we were better off being compact to make them try to find that extra pass. We felt that, if we could stay compact, we'd see it through to half-time.

But it only takes one moment in a game to change everything. We switched off for a split-second, Arteta put a cross in for Arsenal, and Sagna stole in unnoticed and headed a goal back. You could feel the atmosphere in the ground change. Arsenal felt like they were back in the game. They were quick to get the ball and get it going again. They piled on the pressure.

Their second goal was a bit of magic. Van Persie can do that. When he picked the ball up we felt pretty safe – that we had enough bodies there to deal with him. But he just needs a few inches of space to produce a moment and he did. It was a great goal, 2-2.

At half-time I sensed a bit of panic in the changing room. When you're 2-0 up you're not happy to concede two goals, but the game was still there to play for. We should have been focusing on the fact that we're still in the game. It's not ideal, but it's still 2-2, with the second half there to win it. But the team talk was more on the negative.

I think we went out in the second half trying to do too much. We tried to get closer to them, tried to close them down higher up the pitch. For their third goal we got picked off trying to close down in areas they could get out of to break free into other areas. The likes of Walcott and Sagna running freely into spaces can be the difficulty you face when you're playing Arsenal; you're left in the wrong positions and you're chasing a cross, and that's what happened time after time in the second half. Trying to get in their faces, we got picked off. We forgot about playing our own game.

The 5-2 defeat is another bad memory. I'd been there before. You come back in the changing room and you're embarrassed. And it was another personal reminder that I was not the player I had been even a few months before.

People say that Harry successfully defending himself against that tax evasion charge and so putting himself in poll position, everyone thought, for the England management job unsettled the Tottenham dressing room, so ending the great run of play and results. Obviously we were well aware of what was going on, just from papers, the news. But it wasn't something that the manager spoke about. Nor did we ask him. And it wasn't something that we wanted to think too much about either. But it was there, in the papers, in the news. So it was in our minds.

I don't think it affected our football, and it shouldn't have. But subconsciously sometimes these things do. A lot of us looked at the situation and thought the England job is a tough one to turn down. For our money he seemed like the perfect candidate for the job, and I could see him doing well with England. You felt like everything was there for Harry; you looked at his age and you looked at England's previous managers, and you felt that Harry would be the perfect fit.

You could see the appeal, but it was down to him and how he felt. But you hoped that he would still be at the club the following season to take the team further. But it's a decision that will be made based on his own interests. I've seen players make decisions to go: Carrick then Berbatov to Man United, Robbie to Liverpool, and afterwards Luka to Real Madrid.

It was one of those situations you leave in the hands of God and let it play itself out, and what will happen will happen. We just wanted to concentrate on getting the results. Our own pride's involved in this. We wanted to finish in the top four as much for ourselves as for the manager and the fans. We feel that we owe it to ourselves to perform to the very best of our ability.

Any time you go into a game you want to do that. You just hope all the pieces are there to push you in the right direction.

But we went on a difficult run towards the end of the season, and you couldn't put your finger on the reason why. Yes, we lost 3-1 to Man United. But when we then lost 1-0 to Everton, we'd battled the whole of the second half when Everton hardly got out of their end. Jelavic had scored for them in the first half, but the whole second half was us, pressuring and pressuring them. But we couldn't get the goal. Up at Stoke Van der Vaart scored a late equalizer for us. We drew 0-0 with Chelsea, but at QPR, who were fighting for their lives, their ex-Spurs player, Adel Taarabt, scored a free-kick winner. On another day we would have won that game comfortably on the chances we created. That was the difference between this run and earlier in the season: we still were creating chances but now we weren't taking them.

When we just hit that bad patch, some of the performances weren't that bad. We had to try and get hold of the season again before it was too late. Luckily we managed to get better results right at the back end of the season, and to get into fourth came as a bit of a relief.

So, we qualified for Champions League football the following season.

Unless . . .

Unless that season's Champions League final was won by the clear underdog, Chelsea, who, though they finished below

Tottenham in the League, would take their European place the following season as defending champions.

Bayern Munich were the favourites, and we obviously hoped that they would beat Chelsea. But you can't write Chelsea off. They're strong. But we felt we'd done our bit and were confident that Bayern Munich would now beat Chelsea. You do wonder, though, because you see the way Chelsea have got through the tournament. They got through Barcelona, and you wonder how.

I think Chelsea are one of the only teams in England who can play without the ball and get results in Europe. I don't think Man United can have so little of the ball and win games against good teams. Arsenal can't. I don't think Man City can either. Chelsea were the only team that could concede possession against Barcelona, against Bayern Munich, and still be in the game. They stick in there and they get results. So that's why you can never write Chelsea off.

Having said that, this was a good Bayern Munich team, and I was confident they would beat Chelsea. I was watching it in the house with a few friends, Tottenham fans. It was an emotional night. We were jumping up, shouting at the TV. But the moment Drogba scored the goal I sensed the inevitable. And at the end of the game we were left gutted.

But the huge disappointment that, after all that effort and drama, our Champions League place the next season had been taken from us had no bearing on the life-changing decision I now had to face.

A NEW BEGINNING

I love playing football. I would have played as long as I felt I could, but I needed to have a look at the knee situation again. Whatever the problems, I felt I could bounce back as I had so many times before. I always felt that we'd find a way to deal with it next season.

When I suffered the knee injury that Christmas I'd had some scans, and after the end of the season I arranged to sit down with my agents Jonathan Barnett and David Manasseh, and the surgeon, Professor Fares Haddad, after I got back from a short break.

While I was away Jonathan went to see Fares Haddad. When he heard what the surgeon had to say, he then had a conversation with my mum and my girlfriend, Amy. He foresaw that I would need their moral support. When I got back from my brief holiday, I went to see Jonathan with Amy and sat there as he broke it to me that the surgeon had said there's no way I should play any more; he didn't want to see me crippled by my late thirties, needing a walking stick or even a wheelchair.

This was the first time I'd ever been confronted with the

news that now might have to be the time to stop. Even though I knew how my knee really felt, how much in the second half of the season it had deteriorated and restricted my game, what Jonathan had to say was not what I wanted to hear. I couldn't hold back a tear or two as I had to get into my head the realization that maybe I'd played my last ever game of football. That I'd been forced to retire.

But I couldn't just accept the medical verdict without hearing it first-hand. I said I wanted to go and speak to the surgeon myself. We arranged to go down there, and I had a consultation with him.

No medical professional is better acquainted with my knee than Fares Haddad. But at the same time no one knew my knee more intimately than me. I knew that my knee was in a bad way at the end of the season. I wouldn't want to go into a new season feeling the same way. But I tried to cover every angle. How much did he think I could get away with doing? How many games would be safe? Then I assessed the situation myself.

I could not get away from knowing deep inside that, if I was going to come back again, I probably wouldn't be able to do the things I wanted to do. Towards the end of the season, and for the first time in my life, I wasn't enjoying my football. I couldn't move the way I wanted to. I couldn't perform to the standards I'd set myself. And it was making me miserable.

I wouldn't want to do that again. I wouldn't want to put the club in a position where I hoped that I could prove everyone wrong but it became too much. And obviously I did not want to take the risk of putting my knee under further stress which might affect the rest of my life.

It had been five years of coming back from huge problems with that left knee, but I was now at the end of the line. Yes, if I hadn't suffered that blow to the knee halfway through the season, I was confident I could have continued a while longer; I was sure I still had something to give. It was just one of those things.

I came to terms with the decision, and we sat down and spoke to the chairman, Daniel Levy. A little time after, I sat down again for a discussion about making the public announcement of my retirement with the chairman and the club director, Donna-Maria Cullen, and they offered me the ambassador role at the club. They were quick to react to my having to quit playing, which was nice, but I wasn't really sure what being club ambassador entailed. When they outlined what it meant, I was pleased to accept.

We decided that my retirement from playing and taking up the post of club ambassador would be announced at the same time, on 19 July.

I didn't want to be around and contactable that day, I wanted to be away. I didn't want to pick up the papers or see anything on Sky Sports. I wanted to get out of the country and not even pick up the phone; I just didn't want the attention.

I went to Portugal and kept my head down. All the time I was out there it was sinking in more and more that I'd stopped playing the game I love.

When I came back, for the first time in my life I went to work. Playing football never felt like work, it was fun. Playing professional football was a job that was fun. I'd never before in my entire life said the words, 'I'm going to work.' Coming out of my mouth, they still sound funny.

What my role is is something that I've learned as we've gone on. Basically, it's representing the club. But that description in itself is a big umbrella, and in the last year I have done so many different things.

I'm doing a lot of work in the Tottenham Hotspur Foundation with a lot of different kids from tough backgrounds, similar to myself really. These are kids from inner London who might not have any real goals or aspirations. Trying to help them, we've got a project called Skills run by myself and the club in partnership with Haringey Council and the London Boxing Academy. Kids aged from twelve to nineteen can go and participate in various different sports like boxing, football, tennis, basketball, table tennis and dance in the evenings. And during the day there are education facilities there for kids to improve their academic skills. If kids have been excluded or suspended from school, they can down to Skills and catch up, use the computers and not miss out on studying for qualifications. It's all free – the more kids we can get under one roof in a safe environment learning life skills rather than being on the streets like we saw with the riots, the better. Most of the kids down there have been in trouble. The more you're in certain environments, the more likely you are to get yourself into trouble, so the first aim of Skills is to get those kids out of the street environment and in a safe place with kids of the same age and mentors helping them to look forward and find something that they want to do with their lives, a goal.

The mentors are great for the kids because they grew up in the area and they understand how it is for them. I often get down there myself to talk to the kids, and that has been very rewarding. It's important to me to let them know that with focus and hard work they can achieve anything. A lot of kids growing up in Tottenham or similar areas feel that nothing good will ever happen to them because of where they've been brought up. We've got to try to change that attitude. I say to them, I was just like you; I grew up in the East End, a similar environment to Tottenham, and I can tell you from experience that you really do have choices. The opportunity we're offering here is to help you find something you enjoy doing, help you be the best you can, and try to make a career of it. Giving them the knowledge of the choices they have and the support to pursue their talents and passions is important.

We try to promote Skills and get it out there as much as possible. It's done great in the last year; it's really picked up and is growing. Bringing the kids in, the football club obviously has an appeal, and they do a great job in reaching out to the community through the badge and the famous name.

I find that when the likes of myself and other players come in and talk, the kids listen. Sometimes they listen more to people they look up to and see as celebrities than they would to teachers and politicians. Whether it's a footballer or someone in the music industry, their ears prick up. What's been rewarding in this job is that kids are really listening. You can see that they're trying to take on board the message we're trying to send to them.

Two politicians they do listen to are the MP for Tottenham, David Lammy, and the Mayor of London, Boris Johnson. The kids just love Boris; he's a good guy. And I've been around David Lammy when he's told stories about growing up in Tottenham and you can see kids thinking to themselves, wow, he grew up in Tottenham, yet see the level he's got to. His example inspires them to believe that they can get there the same way that I believed when I saw Sol Campbell from my area: if he could get there, I could too. It's exactly the same.

So that's the story I tell them: I was one of the kids who thought, I'm from East London, so nothing good happens to me. But now I've seen first-hand that here's a player from the same area a bit older than me who's done it. So I believed that I could do it too.

It's all about role models, with role models projecting themselves as mentors and examples of finding your talent, finding your ability and working hard at it. Anything you want to do, you do through hard work. You make your own luck. Hopefully that message rubs off on them and they follow their dreams.

We talk to the kids and we listen too, finding out what they need and want. We've seen kids who've come in with no hope of going for job interviews now looking at what they want to do with their lives, really coming a long way in the last year and growing into adults. From being there, a lot of kids are getting into other work within the Tottenham Hotspur Foundation. Some kids have got skills in different areas where they can go on to a different project within the Spurs Foundation.

Aside from this work, I've been to Sweden to see a supporters' club and meet fans, and while I was out there I did some Swedish TV on a Spurs game. I've also been out to South Africa, helping with a bit of coaching with the kids. So every day is different.

The end of the first year in my new job in May 2013 was marked by a gala testimonial dinner, which meant so much to me. Organized with great flair by Lisa Denning and held at London's Park Lane Hilton, it was an event to which loads of my old teammates turned up, suited and booted, to wish me well. Even the Mayor of London, Boris Johnson, found time to bring the full house down with a hilarious and heart-warming speech. I am very grateful not only for all the affection I felt from the fans and friends who were there, but also for their generous support on the night for the good causes I work for in my new ambassadorial role.

On top of my ambassadorial work, I'm doing my coaching badges. It's early days, but I've got the theory down and now I'm doing some of the practical. Doing my badges will be an ongoing thing; I want to do the work properly and learn coaching thoroughly. I don't want to rush it. I want to feel 100 per cent about it. When I'm ready, I'll know it.

Looking further into the future, from time to time I do picture myself as a manager. You think about the pieces you'd need, people you know in the game who would be good in different roles. It's a collective effort, and you need the right team around you. It's too early to say what path I might take into management. When I'm absolutely sure I want to do it and ready for the challenge, I'll push myself at the right opportunity, give it 100 per cent and try to be the best I can.

I'm learning a lot about myself at the moment. In the football world you live in a bubble, and when you come out you can see a bit further. At the moment, in a funny way, I'm learning about life, and I'm continuing to enjoy that experience. I'm seeing what other interests and skills I might have that I never gave myself a chance to learn before. And when I find that next big thing in my life, then I hope to be as passionate about it as I was about football.

And then I'll be all right.

THE NIGHT I TOOK A DIVE

I was never a diver, but when I was clipped in the penalty area one evening at White Hart Lane and the ref himself said to me, 'You might want to go down,' who was I to argue with the man in black? Especially when he's Howard Webb. Just this once, I thought. After all, it is a special occasion.

As captain, I took the pen myself. Back of the net. Sixteen minutes in, and Spurs were 1–0 down.

1–0 down? Huh?

It was a Monday evening, 12 May 2014, and I was leading Ledley's XI against Spurs in a full ground the day after the official end of the League season. With very few players at top clubs staying in one place for long, this was the kind of game you don't see as often as you used to – a testimonial.

My testimonial game, a night of celebration, not so much of me as of my cra as a Spurs player.

Back when this was all first talked about, the thinking was to have a Spurs XI play another club, which is what usually happens at testimonial games. But our problem was timing. With the World Cup coming up and many players at top clubs taking part, making themselves available for a friendly during the preparation stages for Brazil would have been too big an ask. A big-name club but one with few players involved in the World Cup was suggested as opponents. But the idea of inviting Glasgow Rangers didn't sit right with me, because I had no particular affiliation with them; nor was there shared history during my time at Spurs.

So we started looking at other options, and players I'd played with came to mind. We decided on an all-Spurs game, vintage players from various stages of my career against the current squad, including Lewis Holtby back from loan and a lot of up-and-coming players, which I was particularly glad to see, because once upon a time that was me. The youngsters are the future.

But the emphasis that Monday night was on the past. It was a night of nostalgia. The testimonial committee included good friends of mine, Matt Miller and Ramesh Gulrajani, but we needed expert outside help. Testimonials don't come around too often, so finding someone who knew how to arrange things was quite difficult. We got the help we needed from someone with football in her bones. Making it all happen was Di Law, Denis Law's daughter. She'd been involved in testimonials for a while, most recently at Manchester United with Rio Ferdinand, Gary Neville and Paul Scholes, I believe, so she knew just what to do.

So a couple of months beforehand we made some calls, sent

a few texts, and the response I got was great: everyone was keen. More and more people came on board, and at one point I thought I would have too many players.

Even so, there were some guys from early in my career I was sorry not to see. I contacted Gary Doherty – the Ginger Pele! – and he was keen to play but then he got a broken arm. He was gutted, and it was a shame, because we have history together, and I know the fans would have enjoyed seeing him.

One problem we thought we'd have, which turned out not to be a problem, was that my veterans XI were individuals and not a team. We didn't have a single training session together! But on the night it didn't matter. When you see the likes of Teddy Sheringham and Darren Anderton today, they still have that fantastic football intelligence. It was great having some true legends like them and David Ginola and Edgar Davids – great, world-class players from my time in the game.

As for Howard Webb, he was not a bad player either, as he showed on the pitch, and I am so thankful to and appreciative of everyone who took part, from the ref and the players to the tea ladies, ticket sellers and everyone at the club. And, of course, the fans were amazing, not just for buying tickets and coming along but for creating such a fantastic party atmosphere.

Behind it all, of course, there was a serious purpose. In the past the player would pocket all the profits from his testimonial because footballers were much less well paid than they are today and might not have savings to help them through the transition to making a new career. Today, though, the proceeds go to good causes. I was able to help a fund for former Tottenham Hotspur players from way back who'd fallen on hard times, while at the other end of the age range some of the proceeds went to my Skills project through the Tottenham Foundation to take it to the next level with the kids. Some also went to the Bowel Cancer Awareness campaign. Cancer's a big killer - I lost my Nan to bowel cancer and recently also a friend of the family, so the cause is close to me. And then there was the Willow Foundation, set up by the legendary Arsenal goalkeeper Bob Wilson in memory of his daughter Anna, who died of cancer aged only thirty-one. They arrange special days for young adults with serious illness. I went to a Willow Foundation charity event in 2013; it was very touching, and I met some inspirational people, and I knew then I would like to help.

As it all built up before the game, I was getting a bit anxious about it all. I had no idea what the tempo of the game would be and what it would be like to play. But you quickly get the feel of it once it kicks off.

It was difficult for me actually out there on the pitch after two years away from playing. I did a little light training two weeks before, but once out there I realized just how tough football is. For as long as I can remember football has been second nature, but now I could really feel how much the twisting and turning takes it out of your legs. And when that happens you still need to keep your head, your focus, your quality as a player. When your legs are tired, you still need to be able to trap a ball, bring it down and do what you want with it. Suddenly that all felt new to me.

I didn't seek specialist advice before the game because I think I've got pretty good at judging how my body feels and what it's capable of, and I felt I could do it. I had kept up my level of basic fitness since stopping playing and still had control of my body and knew what I needed to do to get ready for a game. I had to be physically prepared.

In the two years since I'd stopped playing my knee had felt better. Without the stresses of football, it felt OK most of the time, with none of the swelling I used to walk around with all the time, only a little stiffness now and again.

At the training ground, the guys who do rehab work with injured players, Nathan Gardiner and Anton McElhone, gave me the run of the place and worked with me in the build-up to the game, and the masseurs greeted me with open arms. It was such a help, and I'm very thankful to them all.

We have great facilities at the new Spurs training centre, and I slowly built up for the game on equipment I never had the chance to use while I was still playing, really up-to-date stuff, which I tested out, like the underwater treadmill to build up my muscles. I was training my feet and legs but, with the water supporting me, only using thirty per cent of my body weight, which is great for my knee. That was the start, then a bit of work in the gym, then outside running, twisting and turning, then finally introducing the ball.

I don't think I'd kicked a football in two years, not even a kick-about with mates. The way the knee is, I couldn't do what I like to be able to do with a ball. The ball itself was the last thing I needed because my goal was really quite simple – it was just to get out there and play without pulling a muscle. And before the game I returned to the routine I had when I played, taking anti-inflammatories. The whole pre-game mood came flooding back to me.

Even after my preparation, once back on the pitch after that time away it was still difficult. It felt like I was right back at the start of my playing career, thrown in at the deep end with a level of intensity that was new to me. And this was a friendly full of retired players, one or two pushing fifty!

Apart from the physical demands, the hardest part was getting your bearings on the pitch, getting used to your position and tracking in your peripheral vision other players' movement around you. Factor out tiredness, and that was the most difficult aspect of playing again as a defender – tracking moves and making the right reaction. You have to see and read the game instantly, when you see a runner, making the right split-second decision to step up, drop back or go with him. When you see the move early and know it's happening, you make the right decision. But when you don't see it early, that's when you make mistakes, when your timing is off. That kind of alertness and awareness comes with playing and training week in, week out, and I found that it had got rusty. So, yes, it was tough, and it brought back to me how tough it is today with the pace of the game. I have a new respect for today's players.

I came off after about an hour, and my body felt tired but fine, my knee only a bit stiff. I didn't think anything more about how my body felt until, boom, after a couple of days, the swelling really kicked in, just like it did when I was playing, when my knee was at its worst forty-eight hours after I'd played. For two weeks after my testimonial it was swollen and quite painful, and after a month still felt a bit stiff, a bit shaky.

Two years is a long time not to play football, but I'm still really only at the beginning of my life after playing.

I've spoken to a number of other ex pros about how to handle life after retiring from the game with all its intensity, pressures and routines. Everyone agrees it's a difficult period, but no one has the same advice. Some say not to rush into anything new too soon and to take time out and do nothing until you have adjusted to your new life. Players like me have had regimented lives since we were kids. We've lived in a bubble with everything done for us even though we've travelled all over the world. You need to get to know yourself, spend time with family, in order to find and fulfil yourself outside that bubble. Others say to throw yourself into another activity as soon as you can. It really is down to the individual. If you're ready when you come out of the game to do something new, that's great.

I've been fortunate to have the best of both worlds. In my job as Spurs Ambassador I both have a brand-new kind of work to do which keeps me busy a number of days a week but also am allowed time to myself.

There is no such thing as a typical week. Some weeks I only have a couple of things to do. Others, I have a full diary of commitments. In a busy week, I will be doing work in the local community, visiting schools, youth centres, the Skills foundation and working with unemployed adults.

I speak to people in groups, but when I go into schools and youth centres, kids seem really keen to come over and talk to me, which is great. I have the chance to speak one-on-one and find out a little bit about them individually. At the Skills foundation I do a lot more one-to-one and always ask what we can do to help move things forward for them. When they have problems outside, they are quite open about it. Here, because what I do is more hands on, we have developed relationships over time as the kids have got to know me personally.

For two years now I've been going into school and youth centres with basically the same message, even if I've added bits over time. The message is simple and based on self-belief and work. You need both. You need to work out what you really want to do, believe you can achieve it and work hard – often really hard – to make that dream a reality.

And then there is respect for others and the value of working in a team. That comes up particularly in the Skills workshop.

You must learn to listen and to communicate in a group. That is a vital skill not just in sport but in life.

On the other hand, I take away a consistent message from the kids. They believe that the area they live in limits their possibilities. I don't believe that, and I tell them. To live in a poor area is a disadvantage, but not one that can't be overcome with self-belief and hard work. There are loads of footballers like me and people who have been successful in many walks of life who are living proof that you can rise above your early circumstances.

I believe in presenting kids with as many options as you can so they can find their route to success. With me there wasn't much around beyond football, but now I see so much talent in music and the performing arts as well as in sport that there are easier ways of pursuing your own path than when I was a teenager.

Then there is my work with the club as an Ambassador. The club has a new sponsorship deal with the Far East-based insurance company AIA, and that means creating relationships in Asia. I have been over to Hong Kong quite a bit, and in June 2014 I spent a week in China, a tough trip with six cities, including Shanghai, Beijing, Nanjing and Guangzhou, in eight days. We'd work full days and only be back in the hotel at midnight, then do it all over again the following morning. It involved a lot of meeting and greeting with business people connected with AIA but also setting up *Football Dream*, a TV programme aimed at kids from fourteen to sixteen based on a football competition. The winners come to Europe to train with Tottenham and Inter Milan – also out there was Edgar Davids.

With China's huge population they have the potential to dominate any sport they choose, but in football there is a lot to be done to realize that potential. The kids I met are enthusiastic, but whether it's something to do with coaching or the culture, I think there is a way to go before we see Chinese players as a real force. Watch this space! With the *Football Dream* programme, I will be in Asia quite a bit doing some coaching and I'll be able to see first-hand how the young generation of players is developing.

I can see China is a beautiful and fascinating country, but on these trips there is little free time to take it all in. I've picked up a few words and phrases. I think I can say in Chinese, 'Hello, nice to meet everyone, I'm Ledley King,' because they seem to understand. It's a very difficult language, but I'm sure I'll pick up a few more words.

For me, it's all good. I'm being stretched in new ways, and as the club grows and explores new opportunities, like in Asia, my job as Ambassador is helping me to develop, to improve, to grow. I'm becoming more confident in talking in front of large groups of people.

Even in things unrelated to work, I'm learning. I could always put a meal together if I had to, but now I'm enjoying cooking and learning more about it. Unlike a lot of footballers, I never played golf, but now I do and quite enjoy it. Tennis too. I love the freedom to try new things. A couple of friends of mine have been skiing, but with my fear of rollercoasters, I'm not sure I'm ready to try myself out on the slopes quite yet!

All the things you miss out on when you play football, I'm now getting. It's a late introduction to the real world – an adult education. I'm becoming a more rounded individual and I'm enjoying it.

Throughout 2013 I worked hard at my coaching with the aim of qualifying. Then the Spurs sponsorship deal with AIA was made, and in 2014, with all the travelling, work on getting my badges became a little stop-start. I need to get another stretch of time where I can rebuild the necessary momentum. In 2014 I was delighted to see Tim Sherwood, Les Ferdinand and Chris Ramsey take their opportunity and do well coaching the first team to a lot of points, and I really value the way they encouraged me to keep going.

For me at Spurs, the possibility of working with the kids as part of the club's coaching structure is very much in my mind. I have a good relationship with young kids and I believe I am a trustworthy person, which is really important when working with a young age group.

Beyond that, I am always reluctant to look too far ahead but, being at Tottenham for as long as I have been, I know that coaching – whether as a head coach or part of his team – is not necessarily a job for life at any one club. It's a fact of the game that once you decide to be a coach, *who* you coach, *where* you coach and *for how long* are not necessarily your choice. Unless you're Sir Alex Ferguson or Arsène Wenger, life as a coach is very unstable. I would love there to be a bit more stability in management, but that is the nature of the game.

It's not just a results business but these days a style business too. To succeed, you don't just have to win but you have to win in a certain way. It's a tough job, but I'm sure no manager would swap it. It's the closest you can get to actually playing, and I feel it offers the greatest potential for me to fulfil myself. In a different way to playing, it tests your skills and knowledge. A coach will get a lot of satisfaction in seeing a player and a team developing in the right direction.

I like the challenge too of working under pressure. Whether you're a player or manager, football makes huge demands, and that is a pressure I have lived with and I find motivates me. I enjoy it! But I might be kidding myself about the degree of pressure on a manager compared to that on any player. It's probably a lot more. Or just a different type.

As a player, I put pressure on myself to perform. I was a thinker. Football was always on my mind, and I was thinking of ways to improve and develop. Any manager will tell you they don't sleep because football is going round and round in their head. All managers want the same thing, to get the best results, and the competition is intense. The best will succeed.

Right now, I believe I would enjoy that competitive pressure as a manager.

To be a young manager and have a great season, with lots of wins, that's great, of course. But I bet you will learn more from your defeats. If you can analyse what went wrong, and how you can improve yourself as a manager and so improve your team, defeat can be the most valuable lesson a young manager can have. Just look at Brendan Rodgers — he has had tough times but come through better and more successful than before. And I hope and believe that André Villas-Boas will have learned more from his time at Chelsea and Tottenham than he did winning everything in Portugal. You have to take the knocks and be able to bounce back. You must believe you can stay the course and turn a bad situation around.

If I was a manager, I would need to have people in my coaching team who see things differently from the way I do, see things I might miss, who take a different view and have minds open to different possibilities. And I would need to listen when they tell me. I might not agree with it, but I need to hear it and think about it. The kind of coach I want to be is one of a team, and not one where it's just all about me.

There is too much pressure to do it all on your own, to work out all the solutions by yourself. Just look at Sir Alex Ferguson at Manchester United. His assistants had a huge influence on him behind closed doors. He was the main man making demands on the team, but on the training ground I bet he had assistants who saw tactics a bit more clearly than he did.

Would I not prefer to be an assistant coach behind the scenes? No. I would want to be in the firing line. I know that Tim Sherwood, coming as he did from an assistant role to be the man under scrutiny from the fans, the board and media, didn't expect as much pressure as there was. But I believe he enjoyed it.

I'm fully aware that, even if I were to become a top manager, I may never manage at Tottenham. Nothing is set in stone. And even if I were to manage Tottenham, there is nothing to stop me getting the sack one day. I've seen it happen to Glenn Hoddle, and, before my time, to Ossie Ardiles, both Spurs legends as players. That's the reality if the results aren't there.

Right now I'm still getting a feel for coaching, and I'm not 100 per cent sure of whether I will take that path. But if and when I am sure I want to be a coach, I will take it step by step and get a feel for my strengths in the job. But enjoyment is the key. The kind of person I am, if I enjoy something, I want to be good at it. As long as I am enjoying coaching, then I will work hard to be the very best I can, and if the opportunities are there, I will take the best one for me at my stage of development.

And then there is Amy. We've been together a while and we will now be tying the knot in 2015. Amy will be a June bride, and – if my knee can take it! – I will carry her over the threshold of what will be our married family home. Sharing the big day in June with my family and friends can't come quickly enough for me, and I am really looking forward to settling down in this new life as a married man. Amy will make me a very happy man, and I can't wait. Wish us luck!

PICTURE CREDITS

Plates

Section 1

Page 1–7
Author's personal collection

Page 8
Top: Action Images/Nick Potts
Bottom: Action Images/David Slater

Section 2

Page 1
Top: Action Images/Roy Beardsworth
Bottom: Action Images/Tony O'Brien

Page 2
Action Images/John Sibley

Page 3
Top: Ben Radford/Getty Images
Bottom: Manchester United via Getty Images

Page 4
Top: Adrian Dennis/AFP/Getty Images
Bottom: Action Images/Richard Heathcote Livepic

Page 5
Top: Shaun Botterill/Getty Images
Bottom: Action Images/Tony O'Brien

Page 6
Top (left): Action Images/Reuters/Toby Melville
Top (right): WNSL/Action Images/Scott Heavey
Bottom: Action Images/Poolpic Livepic

Page 7
Top: Action Images/Scott Heavey Livepic
Middle: Action Images/Jason Cairnduff Livepic
Bottom: Adrian Dennis/AFP/Getty Images

Page 8
Top: Shaun Botterill/Getty Images
Bottom: Action Images/Steven Paston Livepic

INDEX

INDEX

INDEX

INDEX

INDEX

INDEX